THAT OLD BLACK MAGIC

That Old Black Magic

LOUIS PRIMA, KEELY SMITH, AND THE
GOLDEN AGE OF LAS VEGAS

Tom Clavin

CHICAGO
REVIEW
PRESS

An A Cappella Book

Library of Congress Cataloging-in-Publication Data
Library of Congress Cataloging-in-Publication Data

Clavin, Thomas.
  That old black magic : Louis Prima, Keely Smith, and the golden age of Las Vegas /
Tom Clavin. — 1st ed.
    p. cm.
  Includes bibliographical references and index.
  ISBN 978-1-55652-821-7 (hardcover)
  1. Prima, Louis, 1910-1978. 2. Smith, Keely. 3. Witnesses (Musical group) 4. Jazz
musicians—United States—Biography. I. Title.

  ML419.P72C53 2010
  784.4'165092—dc22
  [B]

                          2010015638

Grateful acknowledgment is made to Sony/ATV Music Publishing for permission to reproduce lines from the song "That Old Black Magic" by Harold Arlen and Johnny Mercer; to
Alfred Music Publishing for permission to reproduce lines from the song "Sing, Sing, Sing
(With a Swing)" by Louis Prima; to Joe Lauro and Historic Films for permission to quote
from the documentary *Louis Prima: The Wildest!*; to Garry Boulard for permission to quote
from his book *Louis Prima*; to Mike Weatherford for permission to quote from his book *Cult
Vegas*; and to Simon and Schuster for permission to quote from *Rickles' Book*.

Interior design: Sarah Olson
All photos courtesy of the author unless otherwise credited

Published by Chicago Review Press, Incorporated
814 North Franklin Street
Chicago, Illinois 60610
ISBN 978-1-55652-821-7
Printed in the United States of America
5 4 3 2 1

To Leslie Reingold, for supporting me as a writer and—
the much more difficult task—as a person.

CONTENTS

That Old Black Magic

INTRODUCTION

New Orleans native Louis Prima, a trumpet player and singer molded by Louis Armstrong, was already a grizzled veteran of stage and screen when he met his match. She was barely a performer at all, only half his age, destined for a relatively quiet life of raising kids and maybe singing in the church choir in Virginia. Their encounter was pure coincidence, thanks to an uncomfortably hot day when Keely Smith's family, on vacation, bypassed New York City and caught Prima's show in Atlantic City. But that chance meeting, after some rough years of hammering out the dents and enduring changes in American music, led to the creation of one of the hottest acts in U.S. entertainment history.

Prima and Smith were in the right place at the right time—at the epicenter of an exploding Las Vegas. Their act was instrumental in the transformation of a somewhat sleepy desert oasis into a city of a million lights, one of the most popular entertainment meccas in the world, a place where the biggest stars were paid bags of money to become even bigger stars as live acts and on television shows. Louis and Keely brought together broad comedy with finger-snapping, foot-stomping music that borrowed its energy from the emerging sound of rock 'n' roll. Listening to them, you wanted to jump, jive, and wail, and audiences couldn't get enough. In the years before the British Invasion, their act, "The Wildest," represented what was captivating,

1

romantic, and downright sexy in American music—as much as or even more than Sinatra, Presley, and early Motown.

That Old Black Magic is a showbiz success story with a love interest . . . or is it a love story against a background of showbiz success? In fact, it's both, because the relationship—Keely married the big lug, which added spice to the act—might not have lasted as long as it did without the pulse-pounding dynamic of the stage act, which was like a mating dance done night after night, observed by their backup band, the appropriately named Witnesses. And the act was a lot more appealingly naughty because of the sparks between husband and wife, who got away with jokes and gestures that could have put another couple in jail (yes, even in Vegas).

But maybe the act was too hot to last.

Prima, who would have turned one hundred this year (2010), has been dead for thirty-two years, though you can still hear his braying, eternally cheerful voice on the soundtracks of movies involving Robert DeNiro, Martin Scorsese, and other filmmakers who continue to find him irresistible. Like her husband, Keely had a second phase in her career, but she had to wait many more years for it and survive even rougher times.

But survive she did. Once one of the best-selling songstresses in popular music, Smith was off the entertainment radar screen for decades. Then she performed at the Carlyle Hotel in New York City for the entire month of April 2007. I went, as did many others who wanted to see how she was holding up. She sounded amazing, a singer with a still-strong voice who grabbed the audience right away and held them all night, just like the old days. The critics loved her, and the Carlyle did turn-away business. Keely Smith was back, this time doing it on her own.

This book is about Louis and Keely and the paths they took together and separately. It is also about a certain time in Las Vegas that seems almost quaint now, though it was populated by plenty of mobsters, grifters, pimps and hookers, has-beens, losers, and some wishing desperately to be winners. But what a time it was, when Louis Prima and Keely Smith and the best in show business made music magic into the wee small hours of the night.

—East Hampton, New York, 2010

ACT I

Jump, Jive, an' Wail

1

Yes, they were "The Wildest." It was an hour before dawn on a Friday in the fall of 1958, and Louis Prima and Keely Smith, backed by sideman sax player Sam Butera and the band, were blowing the roof off the Casbar Lounge of the Sahara Hotel, which rivaled the Sands as the most popular nightspot on the booming Las Vegas Strip.

The finger-snapping, toe-tapping ruckus had been going on for over five hours with only a few short breaks. The Witnesses were jamming their way through "The White Cliffs of Dover." Louis lay on the floor, on his back, kicking his feet in the air and blasting his trumpet. Sam crouched above him, blowing every ounce of breath he had through his saxophone. Back up on the tiny stage, Keely—filling out a white taffeta dress in all the right spots and not a strand of her pageboy-style black hair out of place—stood still, staring impassively out at the audience. She had seen it all before, and she'd see it again tomorrow night.

Yet for many members of the audience in the sweltering, smoky lounge, the act was unlike any other that could be found in Las Vegas. No one knew what antics Louis would get up to next, and his sidekick Sam was always there, trying to follow while at the same time leading that tight, tight band. This was the last of five shows that had begun at midnight. In every one, Keely, with those beautiful Cherokee-Irish cheekbones, alternated between belting out one of her signature ballads—"I Wish You Love" and "Come Rain or Come Shine" were real crowd-pleasers—and staring off into space. "I'll stand in front of the piano, lean up against it, fold my arms and stand there for half an hour if I feel like it," she told one of the Las Vegas dailies.

Louis would turn forty-eight in December, but he was like a big black bear in his prime, shouting and scatting and bursting sounds out of his trumpet while jumping around the small stage. All night he did it, all night, with Sam threatening to explode eardrums with his sax and the always-in-motion Witnesses seeming to make up their parts as the night went on.

Their interaction with the audience was nonstop, and the louder and the more ad-libbed the better. Because they were married, Louis and Keely got away with lewd gestures and double entendres that might have gotten other performers arrested (and this included on TV too). *Time* magazine the year before had referred to the act as "relentlessly vulgar," which in Vegas was considered high praise. Radio stations refused to play "Closer to the Bone" because of Louis singing "My slice of Virginia ham is the sweetest meat to eat," and the song was even raunchier live. It was just one of the reasons why the entire show was dubbed "The Wildest."

The stage at the Casbar Lounge was so small that the band's instruments sometimes touched the pitted white tile ceiling, which was barely visible through the foggy layer of cigarette smoke. On the aqua walls in the room hung African masks that appeared to stare at the stage with the same fascination as the audience. As the night wore on, half the audience had become lost in the cigarette smoke. There was only one spotlight and one microphone, but that was enough for a loud and unpredictable show.

Their music had a new sound because they had nothing to lose. Louis and Keely could play whatever they liked. Mixed in the same set could be Dixieland jazz, Benny Goodman, Louis Armstrong, Little Richard and other early rock 'n' roll beats, Charlie Parker, Frank Sinatra, and a gumbo of New Orleans free association. And the audience knew the favorites well, because Louis had made them his own over a long career: "Pennies from Heaven," "When You're Smiling," "Jump, Jive, an' Wail," and, of course, "Just a Gigolo." Though Louis rehearsed his group with a firm hand, once onstage they fed off each other. Louis encouraged spontaneity. Sam Butera explained, "I took what I liked and added my own thing to it."

Louis cavorted his way back to the stage and the song ended, the Witnesses stopping on a dime. The audience shouted and clapped, drowning out the incessant clinking of glasses and snapping of cigarette lighters. Louis laughed, soaking in the ovation, and Sam's grin was wider than the harmonica just a quick reach away in his vest pocket. Her eyes barely moving, Keely scratched an itch under her nose. Then she caught the glance from Louis confirming what was to come next, and she joined him at the mike.

First came Paul Ferrara tapping rapidly on the snare drum. He had created the intro and received the union wage of thirty-five dollars when they'd recorded the song. Next was a dizzy trill from Sam. Then Robert Carter on piano joined in. The crowd exclaimed when Louis sang the first line: "Old black magic has me in its spell."

This was the song they had been waiting for. Sure, the raucous rendition of "When the Saints Go Marching In" always got everyone up on their feet, but that song closed every show, and hearing it meant the night was over. No, they wanted *the* hit, the Louis and Keely version that was blaring out of every radio in the country.

"Old black magic that you weave so well," sang Keely, her smooth voice as sultry as Rosemary Clooney, Peggy Lee, or any singer on the Strip.

Now the whole band was into it—Lou Sino with his trombone, Bobby Roberts on guitar, and Tony Liuzza on bass joining in. Louis bounced up and down on his feet and even Keely had to smile, but she kept her hands clasped behind her.

Louis: "Those icy fingers up and down my spine."

Keely: "That same old witchcraft when your eyes meet mine."

They continued to trade the lines written by Harold Arlen and Johnny Mercer. It truly was a love song, written in 1942 when Mercer was involved with the twenty-something Judy Garland, who just three years earlier had put her indelible stamp on "Somewhere Over the Rainbow" in *The Wizard of Oz*.

"Same old tingle that I feel inside."

"And then that elevator starts its ride."

"Down and down I go."

"Round and round I go."

"Like a leaf caught in the tide."

The song had been a hit for Glenn Miller, reaching number one in 1943. It was a charmed song because it seemed to work for everyone who recorded it—Margaret Whiting, Frank Sinatra, Sammy Davis Jr., Billy Daniels, the Modernaires, and Judy herself. Marilyn Monroe had sung it in *Bus Stop*, a movie released two years earlier, in 1956. But Louis and Keely's version became the all-time classic one. Everyone who heard it knew that. And there was nothing like seeing them do it live in this little casino lounge that fit only 150 people.

Keely's voice rose above the band: "I should stay away but what can I do?"

Louis barked, "I hear your name and I'm a flame."

"Flame, burning desire."

"That only your kiss . . ."

"Put out the fire."

Louis turned and danced away from the mike. Keely swayed rapturously, and the Witnesses turned it up a notch. Abruptly back at the mike, Louis bellowed, "For you're the lover that I've waited for."

"You're the mate that fate had me created for."

"And every time your lips meet mine."

"Baby, down and down I go, round and round I go."

"In a spin, loving the spin that I'm in."

"Under that old black magic called love."

"Ooh, in a spin, loving the spin I'm in."

"Under that old black magic called love."

"In a spin, loving the spin I'm in."

"Under the old black magic called love."

Between bleats of his sax Sam looked out at the crowd. He immediately recognized a half-dozen famous faces: Sinatra in one corner with Dean Martin and Joey Bishop. Debbie Reynolds with a group of people. Tony Curtis and Janet Leigh. For many Vegas performers and celebrities, the night wasn't over until Louis and Keely said so.

"I should stay away but what can I do?"

"I hear your name and I'm a flame."

"Flame, burning desire."

"That only your kiss . . ."

"Put out the fire."

Danny Thomas had told some publication about the Witnesses, "Man for man, pound for pound, it is the greatest musical organization in the world." They sounded like it tonight. Sam might seem tireless, but they took their inspiration from Louis, the man they called the Chief. That came because his wife was part Indian, but mostly because he was the undisputed boss. You do what he says, and you remain in one of the best gigs in show business; you give him grief (especially over money), and you are looking for a job at another casino or in Reno instead of Vegas.

"For you're the lover I have waited for."

"You're the mate that fate had me created for."

"And every time your lips meet mine."

"Baby, down and down I go, round and round I go."

"In a spin, loving the spin that I'm in."

"Under that old black magic called love."

"Ooh, in a spin, loving the spin I'm in."

"Under that old black magic called love."

"In a spin, loving the spin I'm in."

"Under the old black magic called love."

Big finish now, with the band peaking and Louis and Keely singing together into the mike: "Under the old black magic called love!"

The audience jumped to its feet, cheering and applauding. Anyone in the room who didn't was either deaf or dead. Frank bowed to them, and with the hand not holding a cigarette he blew Keely a kiss. What's next, they all wondered. There was almost a groan of disappointment when they heard the opening notes of "When the Saints Go Marching In." The band began a conga line through the crowd, with Louis, of course, leading the way.

That was OK. Many of these folks would be back the next night. There was nothing in Las Vegas like "The Wildest," and in the fall of 1958 Louis and Keely and Sam were at the top of the entertainment game. When even Sinatra bows to you, you're untouchable.

2

———

"There are no second acts in American lives," wrote F. Scott Fitzgerald. He was wrong, surely, in the case of Louis Prima. All Prima needed was an angel like Keely Smith to grant him his second act, and together they made the most of it. Louis and Keely had both a love story and a showbiz success story. And then they blew it.

The story began a century ago. It is surprising that Louis became a jazz musician. Inevitable, too. The surprise is that in his family of men and women one boat ride away from Sicily, the routine occupations were laborers and street vendors. Given his physical gifts, Louis could have done well at either job. The inevitability stems from the musical surroundings of his native New Orleans and, more specifically, the boisterous encouragement of his mother, Angelina, the most profound influence on his life.

New Orleans has most often been associated with the French, but that was not the case when Louis Prima was born there in 1910. The French were the first major immigrant group, and after them came the Spanish. However, immediately before and after the Civil War, Italians dominated the city's immigrant population. According to U.S. Census Bureau figures, between 1850 and 1870 New Orleans was home to more Italians than any other major American city.

The influx continued into the next century, spurred on by the unification of Italy in 1870 and the economic and social problems that followed, which persuaded many people to leave. By the year of Prima's birth the "French" Quarter was 80 percent Italian, the majority of them Sicilian immigrants and their children. A portion of the French Quarter became known as Little Palermo. The Gulf Coast climate was similar to Sicily's, and those leaving Italy sought their fellow expatriates, who had established an expanding community.

"Our grandmothers and grandfathers, they came over here from Sicily and they landed in Argentina," explained Sam Butera in an interview about Prima. "After a few weeks, our grandfathers said this isn't the America we want to be in, so the next port of entry was New Orleans. They knew that there were many Italian Americans in New Orleans."

And there were also a lot of African Americans there. It is estimated that between the end of the Civil War and the dawn of the twentieth century over forty thousand freed slaves and their families walked away from the plantations of Louisiana and Mississippi and sought a new start in New Orleans.

The strongest bond among ethnic groups in the city was between the Italian and black populations. One reason for this was necessity. As the most recent immigrant group—and because of their numbers the most threatening to the white establishment—the Italians had to take whatever jobs they could get. That included working in the sugarcane fields and similar backbreaking occupations alongside blacks. And, like blacks, Italians were the target of blatant discrimination.

The most glaring example occurred in 1891. The New Orleans police chief, David Hennessey, who was often suspected of working both sides of the legal street, was ambushed on the night of October 15, 1890. He was shot several times, and it was reported in newspapers that with his dying gasps he said, "The dagos did it."

Mayor Joseph Shakespeare ordered a roundup, and 250 Italians were arrested. Of these, nineteen were ordered to stand trial, the youngest being fourteen years old. Newspaper accounts insinuated, perhaps for the first time in America, that there was a "mafia" consisting of Italian conspirators, and "Who killa da chief?" became a common taunt.

In the trial the following February, the defendants were represented by Lionel Adams and Thomas Semmes, the latter a descendant of Ralph Semmes, who had captained the *CSS Alabama*, the most famous rebel ship of the Civil War. Members of the jury, none of whom were Italian, found eleven of the accused guilty, although there was no evidence linking them to the murder.

The morning after the verdict, a mob of at least a thousand broke into the jail, and the eleven Italians were beaten and shot before being hanged. It was the largest mass lynching in U.S. history. Italy threatened to declare war, and to appease it and the immigrant population in New Orleans, President Benjamin Harrison ordered that twenty-five thousand dollars be given to the family members of the victims. (In 1999 the incident was turned into an HBO movie, *Vendetta*, directed by Nicholas Meyer and starring Christopher Walken.)

A less violent but more persistent form of discrimination was that Italians along with Jews and blacks could not be members of the "krewes," the organizations that produced the annual Mardi Gras festivities. Italians responded by forming their own organizations, such as the San Bartolomeo Society, founded in 1879 and still in existence today.

Louis Prima was not a philosopher or sociologist, so he never really reflected on the favor done him by necessity and prejudice that placed Italians and blacks in close quarters. At an early age he was influenced by black musicians, and he would always feel comfortable working and socializing with them. He almost lost the most important job of his career in Las Vegas in 1954 because of his anger over the treatment of a black performer. Prima didn't think he was being noble, just human. To him, there was nothing odd about eating, drinking, playing cards, and sharing a stage with African Americans.

Prima was surrounded by an emerging sound that was being called jazz, and Italian musicians were at the center of it. The first jazz recording in the United States was made in February 1917 by Dominic James "Nick" LaRocca and the Original Dixieland Jazz (originally "Jass") Band. The son of immigrants from Sicily, LaRocca had formed the five-piece band the year before. (The first jazz song by a black musician was recorded a month after LaRocca's recording, by Wilbur Sweatman.) The cornet player and his crew became a sort of Johnny Appleseed of jazz, doing shows in Chicago and New York, then going overseas to England and Scotland, performing such LaRocca compositions as "Tiger Rag" and "Sensation Rag."

Emerging black artists rapidly took over the jazz scene. With only a few exceptions, they were the ones touring the country as representatives of jazz performing and composing. Jelly Roll Morton came out of New Orleans and had his best years in New York and Chicago, though his genius wouldn't be fully appreciated until after his death in Los Angeles in 1941. Also gaining attention were Joe "King" Oliver, Buddy Bolden, and Kid Ory.

Then along came the artist who eclipsed them all.

3

Two men who are often cited as the greatest American musical artists of the twentieth century would have significant impacts on Louis Prima. With Frank Sinatra, it wouldn't happen until the 1950s. Prima was a child when he first felt the influence of Louis Armstrong, and it changed his life. Would he have become a musician without Armstrong? Probably, given his surroundings and desire. But he would not have become the Louis Prima who could so captivate and energize an audience.

Armstrong was born on August 4, 1901, in a shack on Jane Alley in New Orleans. His father abandoned his family, which left Armstrong to be raised primarily by his grandmother and, after the age of five, his mother, May Ann, who was only fifteen when he was born. He had a series of "stepfathers," some of whom were his mother's pimps.

Until the age of eleven, Armstrong's experience with music included singing on the street as part of a quartet of friends, blowing through a little tin horn, and staring through cracks in the walls of places such as Funky Butt Hall to watch musicians and dancers. At eleven, he worked for a Jewish family, and, after seeing a five-dollar cornet in a pawnshop window, he saved fifty cents a week until he could buy it.

"After blowing into it a while I realized that I could play 'Home Sweet Home'—then here come the blues," Armstrong wrote many years later.

"From then I was a mess and tootin' away. I kept that horn for a long time. I played it all through the days of the honky tonks."

Even though he was in and out of trouble and was ordered into the Colored Waif's Home for Boys, Armstrong's passion for and mastery of the cornet steadily progressed. He took on a job driving a coal wagon during the day, and at night he prowled the streets of New Orleans, where music blared from open doorways or in some cases the musicians played outside the club to draw a crowd. But especially, there were the parades and the funerals.

"[T]hey dressed in quasi-military apparel, with smart-looking caps, white shirts, and dark pants," wrote Laurence Bergreen in his biography of the musician. "A traditional funeral always began the same way, with the band assembling in the morning, then beginning with stately slow numbers, a few hymns, and the inevitable 'Free as a Bird' to accompany the deceased to his grave; this was a soft, lilting lament mingling sadness and release from mortal cares. Although the New Orleans brass bands played their music soberly and respectfully at the start of a funeral, they soon allowed the rites to take wing and to become a dancing, singing celebration."

Armstrong's favorite performers were horn blowers Freddy Keppard, Buddy Bolden, King Oliver, and Sidney Bechet. He imitated them at first but had begun to improvise when at fourteen he was hired by the owner of a small honky-tonk to play late into the night. Armstrong dreamed of the day that he could be part of a band like his favorites were.

That day came after World War I ended. At seventeen, Armstrong had married a prostitute named Daisy Parker. During their frequent separations, Armstrong hung around a club owned by Tom Anderson, who invited him to play with the house band. Around this time he also was allowed to perform with the Tuxedo Brass Band. Armstrong quickly acquired a reputation as a horn player who never tired, who could almost instantly understand any kind of arrangement, and whom audiences took a shine to because of his crowd-pleasing manner—he invited people to be part of the fun he was having.

His first big break occurred one night while he was sitting in with the Kid Ory band at Co-operative Hall. He was observed by Fate Marable, a riverboat piano player. Marable invited the talented teenager to join his band on the steamer *Sydney*, which traveled up and down the Mississippi.

Audiences outside of New Orleans were exposed to Armstrong's innovative horn playing and infectious laugh. His emerging reputation spread along the river. When not on the steamship, Armstrong played in the cabarets in the city. King Oliver and Kid Ory had formed a band together, and another break for Armstrong came when Oliver succumbed to the siren call of Chicago and Ory asked the young cornet player to replace him, which was a great honor.

By the time he turned twenty, in the summer of 1921, Armstrong was seen as perhaps the best musician in New Orleans, certainly the best horn player, though the singer in him kept trying to get out, as would happen with Prima. "From the beginning, Armstrong's interest in singing and songs equaled his enthusiasm for the cornet and instrumental jazz, the music he more than anyone else would turn into a legitimate art form," wrote Will Friedwald in *Jazz Singing*. "Shortly after leaving the orphanage, in fact, Armstrong composed what would later become the popular standard 'I Wish I Could Shimmy Like My Sister Kate.' Still, for the next dozen or so years of his life, singing took a backseat to the trumpet."

When the piano player Fletcher Henderson, a member of the band backing Ethel Waters, saw Armstrong perform, he urged the horn player to meet him back in New York so they could form a band. Armstrong said that he was not ready to leave New Orleans and his fellow musicians there, or his mother and sister. (Daisy was another matter—her husband lived in fear of the sharp razor she kept handy.) However, in 1922, when King Oliver invited him to join his band in Chicago, Armstrong packed a bag. Four days after his twenty-first birthday, he hopped an Illinois Central Railroad train and embarked on an unprecedented career as a jazz artist.

It could be considered odd that during their lives Armstrong and Prima rarely crossed paths. They were the most famous musicians of the two most musical minority groups in New Orleans, yet they ended up going their separate ways. That they were of different races didn't matter, because Armstrong wasn't prevented from performing with talented white musicians, and Prima played the Apollo Theater and other venues associated with black artists.

Still, Prima repeatedly cited Armstrong as his childhood hero. There is no indication that he ever met Armstrong during their young New Orleans years. Prima said that he gazed through the windows into clubs where Armstrong played, and he saw Armstrong wail away on outdoor bandstands and funerals at which the Tuxedo Jazz Band played.

Prima did not equal Armstrong in musical artistry, but he adapted and developed his showmanship and vocal techniques from the older man. Prima, like Armstrong, was not a polished vocalist, but he was a brazen one who pressed on undaunted and seemed to reach out and hug his audience. Jazz critic Gary Giddins wrote, "'I Surrender, Dear,' which Rudy Vallee called his 'recorded masterpiece,' is one of the grandest examples of [Armstrong's] vocal art, a glossary of expressive tricks. (You can project Louis Prima's whole career from this performance.)" Indeed, Prima copied the master's moves and singing style so well that this, combined with his dark Italian looks, caused him to be refused a job in a midtown nightclub in 1934, when he first arrived in New York City, because the owner thought he was a black performer.

Prima was a white Armstrong, with less artistic talent but more outright showmanship. And there can be no doubt that they both came from New Orleans.

4

During the 1870s, members of the Prima and Caravella families came to the United States from Sicily and settled in the section of the French Quarter known as Little Palermo. The early Primas and their children worked as laborers and operated fruit and vegetable stands. Anthony Prima was born in 1887 and became a big man in the community (literally, at close to three hundred pounds).

He was a gentle giant, a quiet man who was comfortable remaining in the background at social and family gatherings. He went to work every day—when he was twenty-six he became a distributor for Jumbo Soda Pop—and came home to his family. He was known as a soft touch for people in need and appeared not to have a temper.

Louis Caravella was a barber. In his extended family were oyster openers and sellers. His daughter Angelina met and married Anthony Prima while both were still teenagers. They moved into a house on St. Peter Street that over time became one of the more popular gathering spots in the neighborhood of Italians, African Americans, and Jews because of the food and the entertainment. Their first child was Leon, born in 1907.

"My mother-in-law was Angelina, but I called my father-in-law Pop," said Leon's wife, Madeline Prima, in an interview many years later. "He was big, like a Santa Claus, and very quiet. Leon took after his daddy. And Louis took

19

after his mother. She did minstrel shows down at St. Mary's Church, in the Quarter. She sang well. She did a lot of songs, and she loved doing it."

In 1910, over 150,000 people living in the city could trace their family's roots back to Italy. It was a good place to be for Italian American families. The mass lynchings were twenty years in the past, and the families were forming more organizations and making inroads into businesses. In the tight-knit communities much of the socializing revolved around the nearest church. In the Primas' case, this was St. Ann's, four blocks away.

Tony and Angelina's second child, Louis Leo Prima, was born on December 7 of that year. Like Leon, he was baptized at St. Ann's. Within the next few years he would have two sisters, Elizabeth and Marguerite.

The Prima household attracted a lot of visitors, especially on the one day of the week when, after church, neighbors looked for music and laughter. "On Sunday in an Italian home you listen to a lot of Enrico Caruso and a great deal of opera," according to Joe Segreto, who grew up in New Orleans and became Louis Prima's manager in 1961. "It goes well with the pasta and the wine."

The soft-spoken Papa Anthony presided over what his wife provided to family and friends. She was a marvelous and enthusiastic cook, and relatives and friends appeared often at the dinner table. She also liked to sing and tell jokes, so visitors received the complete package.

Louis initially took after his father in being quiet and reserved, but he adored his mother and was fascinated by her showmanship. Though a thin woman, she seemed larger than life. Her opinions and directions were not to be challenged. She handled the family finances and doled out the allowances, even to her husband. Her energy and displays of emotion went beyond the house on St. Peter Street.

Her three children—Marguerite died at age three—were often part of her audience at shows she performed at St. Ann's. Angelina sang and danced in minor productions that she created herself, among them a somewhat risqué one titled "Sadie Green: Vamp of New Orleans." Her motto was "Always smile—people want to see you having a good time." Louis soaked in every moment of her shows that he was allowed to watch.

Angelina had a serious side, too. She insisted that her children continue to attend school as they grew older, and not go to work full-time to help support their families as many Little Palermo children did. As someone who had taught herself to read and write, an education for her children was a priority—and not just for her sons, but for Elizabeth, too, who continued in school until she entered the convent.

Angelina was also determined that her children would make music. Given that they lived in New Orleans, where music was in the air they breathed and perhaps the water they drank, this might seem automatic. But her goal was that her children would learn to play classical music, which was more part of mainstream American culture and . . . well, it was high-class. Like many matriarchs in immigrant families, Angelina was determined that her offspring would be respected and do well financially. She happened to be more formidable than most, so whatever Anthony's views might have been, she spent some of his earnings on piano lessons for Leon and Elizabeth and violin lessons for Louis. The dutiful son, Louis at seven made his first violin out of a cigar box.

They gave recitals. As Leon remembered in the documentary *Louis Prima: The Wildest!*, released in 1999, "When we were kids, I played the piano and Louis would play the violin, and Sister Maryann [Elizabeth] played the piano too." Papa Anthony smiled benignly, but what mattered most to Louis was Angelina's effusive approval. From an early age, he learned how to win love from his audience.

But Angelina's vision of her children—or at least her sons, since Elizabeth found a different calling—going on to college and maybe playing with orchestras was derailed, ironically, by music. The lure of jazz and blues sweeping through the clubs and even some of the churches in New Orleans proved to be too strong for Louis and his brother.

"We used to listen to the black fellows that would play," Leon said. "Trucks came along, and the bands on them would play."

"We lived in what was called 'Back-a-town,' primarily a colored neighborhood," Louis recalled in a 1970 interview for the New Orleans Jazz Museum. "We used to follow those colored bands on their trucks around. They would congregate in the neighborhood on Sunday afternoons. And we lived near a cemetery, so we watched all the funeral parades marching in and out."

Louis was a little more adventurous than Leon. "Louis told me that as a child, he also went and stuck his head in the little black churches which were very near where he was raised, and see all of that excitement that was part of the worship," said Segreto in the 1999 documentary.

Angelina didn't stand a chance. Louis and his brother were adolescents in a musical environment that not only held a major city in its grip but was also changing the culture of the country.

"My brother Leon started it all," Louis said in a 1974 interview. "He played piano. In school they made me leader of the orchestra because I played the violin, but I followed Leon and the boys in his jazz band around. I wasn't making it with the violin because I was playing all of the 'long hair' stuff."

For much of his life, Louis eschewed the "long hair" stuff and gave his audience the popular tunes they wanted. One of his slogans was "Play pretty for the people." He was about to learn how to do so.

5

For much of its history, the music of New Orleans remained regional. That was about to change, and many of the major cities in the United States were going to experience what that hybrid music was all about. Television in most American homes was still decades away, but in the 1920s the New Orleans sound spread out because of radio and the native musicians who took their songs, performing styles, and stories on the road.

"If you look at Canal Street in the midst of a Zulu parade in the 1920s, what you're going to see is white, black, colored, Latino, in other words, the entire spectrum of ethnicity right there on the street, waiting for King Zulu to come down, waiting for the music," says Bruce Raeburn, head of the Hogan Jazz Archive at Tulane University in New Orleans. "The jazz bands are making music for themselves because in New Orleans music is not a luxury, like it is in most American cities. It's a necessity. This is where New Orleans musicians excel."

It was this spirit, or life force, as much as the brilliant music, that Louis Armstrong introduced to the rest of America. He was ready to be the messenger.

"Armstrong's reach for urban sophistication in New Orleans had prepared him well for Chicago and New York," wrote Thomas Brothers in *Louis Armstrong's New Orleans*. "Was playing like this produced independently in any other southern city? It is highly unlikely. Oliver, Bechet, Armstrong, and their fellow New Orleanians sounded completely fresh when they traveled around the country because no place else had the same social and musical history, with all its layers of patronage and practice and its sequential development, the heyday of which coincided with the first twenty-one years of Armstrong's life."

Armstrong had played with King Oliver's Creole Jazz Band for a year and then joined the Fletcher Henderson Orchestra. He was also recording as a sideman to Clarence Williams and Bessie Smith as well as Oliver and Henderson. Then, for three years beginning in 1925, Armstrong made the "Hot Fives," the nickname that has been given to a series of records with a small group that "are by general consensus the most influential of Armstrong's accomplishments and quite likely the most significant body of work in all of jazz," according to Will Friedwald in *Jazz Singing*. "Here he changes the face of jazz on every conceivable level. Even before 1928, Armstrong's achievements begin to elevate from a purely musical plane to a social one, as he launches the shifts in the music that would enable it to become both a high-brow art form and an international pop entertainment."

The latter would become especially important to Louis Prima. Armstrong blazed a trail of jazz–popular song fusion (and, later, comedy) that Prima traveled enthusiastically. Both men would be ridiculed and even dismissed by some critics for straying off the jazz reservation into pure entertainment territory. While this sometimes angered Armstrong, Prima couldn't care less, and pleasing his audience without worrying about aesthetics became his North Star.

That Armstrong was changing the substance and to some extent the face of American music in the early to mid-1920s was perfect timing for Prima. Back in New Orleans, Angelina's insistence that her children not go to work so that they could concentrate on school and homework and classical music led, ironically, to Leon and Louis having more time than most youngsters to roam the streets to seek out the hottest music and the best performers in the French Quarter and other neighborhoods. The brothers, in their early teens, could not get into the nightclubs, but they could catch glimpses of the stage through doorways, and many times it was enough to stand outside and listen.

For two impressionable adolescents, the music of Haydn, Mozart, and Bach could not possibly compete with the sounds of homegrown Dixieland jazz being altered and energized by African American blues and gospel. Despite his shy demeanor, Louis was a restless youngster, and the music simply made him feel that he wanted to dance and that he could connect to others through music. A violin just wasn't going to do that for him. And, he couldn't help but notice, women went wild over horn players.

Leon was the first to defy Angelina. He told his mother that he would no longer take piano lessons. Worse, he was going to learn how to play the cornet. That is what Armstrong and Bechet and Oliver played, and audiences loved them. Piano was fine for ragtime, but that music was out and jazz was in. Angelina was aghast, but Leon was adamant. Papa Anthony most likely had no opinion on the matter and just wanted peace in his house.

Soon after, Louis made the same declaration. This time, however, Angelina prevailed over the wishes of her less-stubborn younger son, and Louis continued with the violin, or what he preferred to call a fiddle. Though his heart wasn't in it, he did want to please his mother, and he couldn't help trying to be a very good musician. He became head of the class band at Jesuit Junior High School, and in 1921, at age ten, he won the ten-dollar top prize in a fiddle contest.

By the time Leon was sixteen, he had gotten so accomplished as a cornet player that he began to be hired to play with bands in local nightclubs. It only increased Louis's envy and frustration when he listened to Leon practice in the St. Peter Street house, then snuck off to see his older brother perform in the same clubs where he had gotten looks at his idols, who were black, white, and everything in between. Louis was twelve years old and feeling left behind.

The following year, in 1923, Leon, though still a schoolboy, spent seventy-five dollars on a new horn, a trumpet. That his old cornet sat idle in Leon's closet or under his bed had to feel to Louis like a large bag of uneaten candy just going to waste. The next summer, when he was thirteen, a golden opportunity presented itself. Angelina went away for several days to visit relatives, and Leon was on tour with a band.

"When I went on the road, I left an old trumpet at home and stayed out about a year or so, and when I came home, Louis was blowing the trumpet," Leon recalled. "And he was blowing it real good."

It is not known exactly how Angelina reacted when she returned home to find Louis, immediately addicted, learning to make a different kind of music. That summer, however, Louis was put to work in his mother's small shop selling flavored ice shavings and on his father's horse-drawn wagon delivering Jumbo Soda Pop. If the plan was to dissuade Louis from playing the horn, it failed. The combination of playing jazz and puberty was too powerful for the boy to resist. In the summer of 1924, Louis Prima was transformed.

The retiring Papa Anthony personality was gone—or at least it retreated inward—and the flamboyant Angelina side emerged and took lifelong control. At thirteen, Louis Prima became a bandleader, and with a few early exceptions he remained one for fifty-one years.

The group of six classmates (plus himself) that Louis pulled together was called—directly and sensibly—Prima's Kid Band. He was clearly the leader when they played on street corners and at special events, as he was the one out front singing and dancing. His initial efforts were pure imitations of the performers he admired, especially Armstrong, but as the months went on his act became more of an improvisation—he moved the way the music moved him. At the same time his technical skill as a horn player improved. He wore a colorful vest and parted his dark hair in the middle, a style he wore into the 1940s, or as long as he had enough hair.

"Everybody kept telling me how good he was," Leon told writer Garry Boulard in 1984 about the period after he returned to New Orleans from the tour. "So the next time he played, I went to see him, and, I gotta tell you, he was good. He was jumping all over, and the audience loved it."

His new career made school even more boring by comparison. Louis attended Jesuit High School, but that wasn't working out, so he transferred to Warren Easton High School when he was fifteen. A reconstituted band he formed there had another unsurprising name, the Eastonites.

School took more of a backseat as Louis led his band from one street to another, performing wherever they found a good place to set up. He also tried to book the band into French Quarter clubs, but such gigs were rare because of the ages of the band members and Angelina's objection that he would fall under unwholesome influences. Finally, at seventeen, in the spring of 1928, Louis left school. The closest he ever got to college was forming a group called the Little Collegiates that played in neighborhood theaters and could command as much as two dollars a night.

It was time to stop pretending. Louis was not going to take over his father's soda distribution business or become a local laborer or start up any kind of business, and sure enough he wasn't going to have an academic career. He had been bitten by the jazz bug, and it was time to devote himself to being a professional musician.

6

———

Louis Prima became a professional musician when he joined the musicians' union in 1928. The union in New Orleans was all about trying to get gigs, and this meant primarily playing some theaters like the Saenger on Canal Street. The problem was, if you wanted to play jazz you might find yourself a little out of place in some of these theater pit orchestras.

But Louis didn't worry about that; he just wanted to play, and the more the merrier. Radios in New Orleans were tuned to the national networks NBC and CBS, which broadcasted the music of full orchestras. Local musicians knew that performers like Louis Armstrong, Jelly Roll Morton, and others were now members of such orchestras or were in the process of forming their own. Orchestras formed elsewhere—such as those led by Guy Lombardo, Paul Whiteman, and Duke Ellington—were beginning to put New Orleans on their tour itineraries or at least were being heard on the radio stations. To keep up, the city had to spawn its own orchestras, which was good news for a young man in the Roaring Twenties looking for work and plenty of it.

Ellis Stratakos hired Prima when he was only eighteen to play trumpet in his orchestra. This could have been a terrific opportunity for a teenager, but alas, the orchestra wasn't that good. When it tried its fortunes on a trip to Florida, few people showed up to listen and dance. The orchestra disbanded, leaving Louis and the guitarist Frank Federico, a former schoolmate, stranded. The two friends subsisted on the citrus fruits that littered the roadsides as they hitched their way back to New Orleans.

Like Armstrong, Prima found a break by being signed aboard a steamship. The steamship *Capital* was berthed on Canal Street, and Louis became part of its band. This too didn't last very long, and it resulted in another relationship that was not destined to be an enduring one.

Louise Polizzi and her girlfriends liked to dance to the band on the ship, and Louis liked to watch Louise dance. They began to see each other off the ship and dated for six months.

"He was very different," she told Boulard in a 1984 interview. "He wasn't like people thought. He wasn't always happy and dancing around. Sometimes he'd be very sad. He'd cry very easily if something was bothering him." She added an observation that would be repeated for the rest of Louis's life: "He didn't even have very many close friends, although he knew a lot of people."

Louise and Louis were married on June 25, 1929, possibly on the sly, because the ceremony was performed in Jefferson Parish by a justice of the peace. Apparently accepting the fact of it, even though her youngest son was still only eighteen, Angelina orchestrated a more official ceremony at St. Ann's. The newlyweds took up residence in the Prima household, which meant that Louise too came under Angelina's jurisdiction.

Shortly before his next birthday, Louis, now with a wife to support, was hired by Joseph Cherniavsky to play trumpet in his orchestra, which had an ongoing engagement at a gambling house in a suburb of New Orleans. Even better news was that Louis was encouraged to play to the audience and improvise. The bad news was that he became so good at it that audiences wanted to see and hear more of him and less of the rest of the orchestra.

"I happened to be one of the extra reed men that they wanted in there," recalled Dave Winstein, a friend of Prima's. "And Louis was one of the trumpets. But Cherniavsky never did like Louis's style of playing, so he gave Louis the regular two weeks' notice that is required, and this young man was practically in tears when he said one of these days this guy is going to feel sorry. He said, 'I'm going to make it. He fired me, but he's going to be sorry he fired me. I'll be bigger than he was.'" That, of course, became a huge understatement.

Prima had no trouble finding other gigs. The arrival of the Depression did not mean that New Orleans would lose its music. In the city, orchestras and new venues kept springing up. It helped too that his brother, Leon, was also becoming successful. He put together the Prima-Sharkey Orchestra, one of the most popular big bands in New Orleans. Apparently because of its popularity, it was able to get away with including both black and white musicians, though that was against Louisiana's segregation laws. Leon also opened a dance pavilion and after that the Avalon nightclub. Louis frequently played there when he found himself between jobs.

Louis's increasingly vibrant performances caught the attention of Lou Forbes, who led the orchestra at the Saenger Theatre. He hired the nineteen-year-old in 1930. The Saenger was also known as the Florentine Palace, and it showed movies all afternoon and evening. Between films the orchestra played, with some of the members jumping out to dance in colorful costumes. This was a golden opportunity for an irrepressible young man.

"He showed you everything there was to know," said drummer Godfrey Hirsch about Forbes in *Louis Prima—The Chief*, a 1983 documentary produced by WYES-TV in New Orleans. "He did the same thing for Louis."

"I got a lot of my knowledge and picked up a lot of pointers from Lou," Prima said in the 1970 interview. "He was quite a showman."

In addition to blowing the trumpet, Prima played a variety of roles in musical-comedy skits that Forbes choreographed—a policeman, a hick from the sticks, even a chicken. He began to be reviewed favorably in the city's newspapers as someone who played a mean trumpet and had an anything-goes stage persona. (Angelina clipped the reviews out and put them on display for family members.) By the spring of 1932, he was billed second only to Forbes himself.

According to bandleader Woody Herman in *Louis Prima: The Wildest!*, "When I first arrived in New Orleans in 1932, I was a saxophonist with the Tom Gerun Band of San Francisco. One of the new young people who was making a big impression locally was Louis Prima. He was a new kind of entertainer. Lots of energy. And he could turn a word and get a laugh anytime he wanted."

One of Prima's more popular engagements outside of the Saenger Theatre was at the Beverly Gardens on River Road, and it involved a black youngster named Earl Palmer. Palmer later became a drummer who worked in and led bands in New Orleans. After moving to Los Angeles he became the studio drummer on dozens of seminal rock 'n' roll hits, including Sam Cooke's "Shake," Ritchie Valens's "La Bamba," Eddie Cochran's "Summertime," and most of the hits by Little Richard and Fats Domino. Charlie Watts of the Rolling Stones and Max Weinberg of the E Street Band are among the many drummers who have cited Palmer as a powerful influence.

But in 1932 he was only seven years old and trying to survive by singing and dancing on street corners. Prima hired him for five dollars a night plus tips for a short skit: while Prima paused between songs to talk to the audience, Palmer wandered out and pulled on his jacket.

"Go away, boy, you're bothering me," Prima said. "I'm trying to talk."

Palmer continued to pull on Prima's jacket until, exasperated, he shouted down at the child, "What do you want?"

"Daddy, Mama wants you on the telephone!"

In *Backbeat*, his autobiography, Palmer wrote, "Of course, the crowd roared. Prima says out of the side of his mouth, 'Here, kid, take this and beat it.' Slips me five or ten, like he doesn't want the people to know."

Unlike some residents of New Orleans who were feeling the impact of the Depression, Prima seemed set for years. He could expect his local fame to grow, along with his salary, which was sixty-five dollars a week at the Saenger. He supplemented that with late-night gigs in clubs. The money allowed him to dress like something of a dandy, begin a lifelong obsession with horse racing, and provide for a pregnant Louise.

But after the birth of his daughter Joyce in 1933, Louis became restless. New Orleans was a pretty big pond, but he envied the fish in bigger ponds. The airwaves were carrying new bands formed by Benny Goodman, Guy Lombardo, and the Dorsey Brothers in addition to the established orchestras broadcasting from New York and Chicago. There were also the examples of Armstrong, Morton, Oliver, and others who, it was believed, were enjoying fame and fortune in the bigger venues.

Lombardo provided a temptation that proved to be too strong. He and his band, which included two of his brothers, Lebe and Carm, arrived in New Orleans for several concerts as part of the 1934 Mardi Gras celebrations. Their father had also emigrated from Sicily, but to London, Canada. Guy's band had become one of the more popular ones in the United States, too, and this was its debut in the Big Easy.

"Everywhere, especially on Bourbon Street, there were small clubs and in them were fine musicians," Guy Lombardo recalled in *Auld Acquaintance*, his autobiography. "It was springtime and warm enough so that the doors of the clubs were open. Up and down the street, sounds poured out, sweet, penetrating, Dixieland and improvised jazz. One night, walking alone, I heard the sound of a trumpet, different and more piercing than any I had experienced. I walked into the tiny club, which was almost empty. On the bandstand was an olive-skinned trumpet player, hardly more than a boy. He was leading a four-man group and a girl vocalist sat beside him. They were putting as much into the show as if the place overflowed with patrons. And the trumpet player so impressed me I ran back to the hotel and got Carm and Lebe out of bed."

He dragged his brothers back to the club, and they were also entranced by Louis Prima. Playing a trump card to visitors from out of town, he invited the Lombardo brothers to his house for dinner the next night. They chatted amiably with Papa Anthony while sampling dish after dish of Angelina's cooking.

"We came to hear Louis every night we could and I finally asked him if he would like to come to New York," wrote Lombardo. "I was sure I could find a job for him; I hadn't heard this type of music in the big town. I had one place in mind for him, a well-known nightspot on Fifty-second Street, Leon and Eddie's."

It didn't seem to matter to Louis what Louise thought about a move to New York. Indeed, she might have even assumed that she and her daughter would go with her husband. But as far as Louis was concerned, he was going alone. The only question was whether his mother would let him go at all. His wife and child were nothing compared to the formidable Angelina.

It took months to win her over. She thought Louis should be content with a life in New Orleans that appeared enjoyable and increasingly successful and that he should stay put with a wife who could give her more grandchildren. And, of course, Angelina couldn't stand the thought of being without the apple of her eye. But as the summer turned into fall, she knew she had to let him go. His talent, energy, and showmanship needed a bigger stage.

As Louis Armstrong had done twelve years earlier, with a case carrying a new trumpet under one arm, in September 1934 Louis Prima hopped a train north and left his family, his wife and child, and his friends behind. He was only twenty-three, yet he had the confidence to believe that it would not take him years of struggle to achieve fame.

7

_____

At first, it wasn't an easy transition to New York City. When Guy Lombardo had returned there, for his orchestra's debut at the Waldorf-Astoria, he went to see Eddie Davis, co-owner of Leon and Eddie's. Davis thought he could use a five-piece band, and he was willing to believe that maybe there weren't already enough trumpet players from New Orleans around.

When Prima finally arrived, Lombardo took him to see Davis. After a few minutes of talking, Davis took Lombardo aside and told him that the union would not allow him to fire the five-piece band he already had, so there was no room at the club for Prima's group. Lombardo was very embarrassed. To make up for it, he booked Prima and his band members into rooms at the Waldorf and asked a friend to try to find work for them at other clubs. After the gig at the New York hotel, the Guy Lombardo Orchestra left for an engagement at the Cocoanut Grove in Los Angeles.

It wasn't until weeks later that Davis told Lombardo the truth: the club owner hadn't hired Prima because, he said, "I thought he was colored, and I just couldn't take a chance on losing customers."

Lombardo later explained, "The management of hotels and the night-club owners simply refused to break the color line, fearing financial consequences. Many of the best bands in the country were black—Duke Ellington, Louis Armstrong, Cab Calloway, Fletcher Henderson—but job opportunities were difficult to find outside of Harlem. Eddie Davis, on first seeing olive-skinned and swarthy Louis Prima and knowing that he came from New Orleans, had simply assumed he was a black man."

Prima probably didn't think so at the time, but he was a rather fortunate man. For four years, more than half the musicians in the country had been out of work, which would not have been a good environment for a young man with a horn just arrived in New York from New Orleans. But in 1934 the effects of the Depression were mitigated to some extent by the repeal of Prohibition the year before. Nightclubs didn't have to hide in back alleys hoping that customers would come in to drink bootleg whiskey. Now they could serve alcohol as legitimate operations that also provided music.

"The repeal of Prohibition at the end of 1933 radically altered the character of Manhattan's night life for the privileged few who could still afford one," wrote Ross Firestone in *Swing, Swing, Swing,* his biography of Benny Goodman. "The speakeasies closed their doors and immediately reopened as nightclubs, some of which—El Morocco, The Stork Club, '21'—affected an air of genteel exclusivity that belied their less reputable origins."

Because of Lombardo, who felt responsible for Prima uprooting himself (though he was more than ready to go), Louis was able to get gigs here and there so he could at least eat and afford a hotel room. In addition, a low-budget company, Brunswick, invited Prima to bring his five-piece group to its studio to record several songs.

The songs that came out of the Brunswick sessions made Prima only a few bucks, but he received some exposure as a bandleader and arranger as well as a composer and trumpet player. More important, the sessions caused Prima to hire Pee Wee Russell to play clarinet in his band, which was called Louis Prima and His New Orleans Gang. Sidney Arodin, a New Orleans clarinetist who had been part of the Gang, had just joined forces with another New Orleans trumpet player, Wingy Manone, and Louis was delighted to find Russell, who had spent some time in Leon Prima's band, available. Until Prima recruited Sam Butera twenty years later, Russell was the best sideman he had.

"I was fortunate in having Pee Wee Russell with me," Prima told an interviewer. "[He was] the most fabulous musical mind I have known. He never looked at a note. But the second time I played a lick, he'd play along with me in harmony. The guy seemed to read my mind."

Charles Ellsworth Russell Jr. had been born twenty-eight years earlier in St. Louis. Like Prima, he played the violin as a child. But when he was twelve, and the Russell family was living in Oklahoma, his father took him to a show featuring the Louisiana Five, a New Orleans band with Alcide "Yellow" Nunez on clarinet. The next day he begged his parents for the instrument. By the time he met Prima in 1934, Russell was considered second only to Benny Goodman in clarinet players among most critics, if he was considered second at all.

"No jazz musician has ever played with the same daring and nakedness and intuition," wrote Whitney Balliett in a *New Yorker* profile of Russell. "He took wild improvisational chances, and when he found himself above the abyss, he simply turned in another direction, invariably hitting firm ground."

For the next several months, Prima made his first classic records. Recorded in one take was "The Lady in Red" featuring a trumpet-versus-clarinet duel, which would become a trademark of Prima and Russell's work together for the next two years.

Perhaps most fortunate for Prima was the emergence of Fifty-second Street as a jazz mecca. Leon and Eddie's at 33 West Fifty-second Street was joined between Fifth and Sixth Avenues by Jack and Charlie's 21 Club and the Onyx Club as the area evolved into "Swing Street."

"In its flourishing decade (1935–45), The Street served as the launching pad for more singers, more hit songs and more instrumentalists than any of the country's entertainment centers—Rush Street in Chicago, Bourbon Street in New Orleans, Beale Street in Memphis, and Central Avenue or The Strip in Los Angeles," wrote Arnold Shaw in *The Street That Never Slept*.

It was a new nightspot, the Famous Door, that put Prima on the musical map as a jazz artist and quickly established him as one of the hottest acts in New York. Jack Colt, a businessman from Connecticut, found a few investors—among them bandleaders Jimmy Dorsey and Glenn Miller, trombonist and future pop-eyed comedian Jerry Colonna, and composer Gordon Jenkins. Colt also reached into his own pocket to come up with $2,800 to open a club one door west of Leon and Eddie's, at 35 West Fifty-second Street. The concept was to provide a place for other musicians to come and listen to the latest jazz when their own gigs were done. The signatures of the owners on the door next to the bar, not the front door, were what gave the club its name.

In March 1935, Colt hired Louis Prima and His New Orleans Gang, which by this point was a well-rehearsed band, with Prima and Russell pushing each other during their dueling solos. Opening night—which, fortuitously, was the night after the Onyx Club up the street burned down—was at first a disaster. Only a handful of customers showed up. Prima was not used to big crowds in clubs in New York anyway, so he and his band went ahead and performed as though they were at Carnegie Hall. At eleven o'clock, Colt was too depressed to stay and watch, and he went for a walk.

While he was gone, several things happened: (1) The music of Prima's band wafting out onto Fifty-second Street attracted people out strolling after dinner or the theater; (2) as originally intended, musicians who had finished their own shows were now on the prowl for something different; and (3), as people gathered at the front of the club, other people saw them and, not wanting to miss out on whatever was going on, joined them. The crowd swelled.

Colt returned to find patrons literally fighting to get in and his bartenders borrowing booze from neighboring clubs to meet the suddenly daunting demand.

"The Famous Door caught on that first night, with the customers it was opened for, and caught on soon thereafter with the customers who were never expected," wrote Robert Sylvester in *No Cover Charge*. "Society came. Broadway came. Everybody came. The Door brought to first fame such arch musicians and singers as The Ink Spots, Bunny Berigan, Red Norvo, Max Kaminsky, Billie Holiday, Teddy Wilson, Bobby Hackett, Wingy Manone, Joe Marsala and dozens more. . . . Swing Street was in business."

But first among the first was Louis Prima. He and Russell—paid sixty and forty dollars a week, respectively—and their sidemen became a sensation. "When Prima plays there on Fifty-second Street, it starts this big breakthrough, this avalanche of interest in Fifty-second Street, and it really establishes that venue as the street of jazz as it became, and it also established Prima as kind of a trendy in thing at that point," reported jazz historian Will Friedwald in the documentary *Louis Prima: The Wildest!* "That's Prima's first burst of fame."

Like a burst of fireworks, Prima and his act in New York City were colorful and thrilling—and just about as brief.

8

———

Prima already rehearsed relentlessly when he was hit with sudden success. Throughout his career he drove himself and his band hard, dictating every arrangement and dance move, though later on, with the Las Vegas act, he allowed for improvisation onstage. He made sure that the people playing behind him received credit, but they had to keep earning it. One time Pee Wee Russell was late for a rehearsal, and for the next week onstage at the Famous Door, Prima introduced everyone in his band except him.

Night after night, Louis Prima and His New Orleans Gang packed the club, helped by items in newspaper columns by Walter Winchell, Ed Sullivan, and others. For the Famous Door gig he had created a slogan, "Let's have a jubilee!" He adapted a song for his band with that title, written by W. Alexander Hill and Irving Mills. It further enhanced his reputation as a flamboyant showman that, to close the club at 3:30 A.M., Prima had the band swing into "Let's Have a Jubilee," which had also opened the show, and in New Orleans style he led them off the stage, through the audience, and out the door to parade down Fifty-second Street.

Eddie Davis across the street had plenty of time to regret his decision to reject Prima, but he was consoled by the cliché "A rising tide raises all boats." With more people flocking to Fifty-second Street to check out the new nightlife sensation, there were plenty of patrons to go around. If you couldn't get into the fifty-seat Famous Door, you could just step into Leon and Eddie's.

However, many women wouldn't settle for another club. They adored Louis Prima. He adored them back for his entire life. "Apparently, according to all eyewitness testimony, Prima was a ladies' man for his whole career," said Friedwald. "He had five wives and Lord knows how many affiliations, as it were."

"Louis was the kind of guy who could engender a little romance with the ladies, you know?" Joe Segreto said in the Prima documentary. "He was a big, good-looking guy, and he was a star. Louis caused a lot of excitement with the audience, and I guess some of that spilled into the interest after the show."

According to Sam Weiss, a well-known club owner at the time, "When [Prima] shouted, 'Let's have a jubilee,' a lot of those sex-starved dames would practically have an orgasm. I think they thought he was shouting, 'Let's have an orgy,' in that hoarse, horny voice of his."

"I actually saw women pass out," reported the guitar player Frank Federico, his New Orleans friend who rejoined Prima in New York. "Just blow their top in the Famous Door there in New York."

"What Louis was bringing was a kind of special verve that he had, not only as an instrumentalist but as a vocalist particularly," says Bruce Raeburn. "He had his own style."

In addition to being in close proximity to women, success for Prima meant rubbing elbows with mobsters.

"The reality of the situation, particularly as it affected jazz musicians between 1880–1940, requires that these hitherto unpublicized admirers and well-wishers be discussed for what they were and what they did," wrote Ronald Morris in *Wait Until Dark*, his study of the nightclub scene in New York. "I am referring to that legion of underworld characters known in the Broadway vernacular as mobsters and racketeers. I am also referring to their sponsorship of jazz, an activity without which the artists themselves would have shriveled up and died."

Prima was an especially attractive draw for mobsters. He was of fully Sicilian descent, and looked it. He and his group were one of the hottest acts in town, and he was an entertainer on his way up. Yet there is nothing to indicate that Prima courted gangsters or wanted their approval or even attention. In fact, he had a few reported run-ins with mob tough guys, and this may have been a reason why he left New York abruptly for Los Angeles. One, according to Robert Sylvester, took place at the Famous Door when a hit man known as Pretty Boy Amberg slugged Prima because he didn't play a requested tune. Most musicians, white as well as black, knew that Duke Ellington had been the victim of a kidnapping attempt in 1931 and that he carried a .38 revolver whenever he was not onstage.

From his days of playing in clubs in Chicago, Russell was even more familiar with the underworld. He claimed to have repaired tommy guns for mobsters and disposed of pistols for them in Lake Michigan. There must have been some truth to his assertions about close ties to the mob. According to several accounts, Prima and Russell were confronted one night by a couple of men with knives who demanded protection money. Russell contacted Lucky Luciano, who dispatched Amberg and a chauffeur to drive the two musicians from their hotels to the Famous Door and back after the show. Prima and Russell were not approached again.

Only a year after Prima was not hired to play at Leon and Eddie's because of the belief that he was black, Prima's skin color gave him an advantage over many other musicians in New York—he was welcome in both of the jazz hubs in the city. He had quickly become royalty on Fifty-second Street, but he and his band were embraced uptown, too. The area in and around Harlem boasted such jazz and dance music venues as the Plantation Club, Kit Kat Club, 101 Club, Hoofer's Club, Bert Hall's Rhythm Club, the Cave, Brandy Horse, and others. Ellington, Count Basie, and Cab Calloway were the bandleaders mixed audiences wanted to see.

The publication *Billboard* even referred to Prima and his "jam band" as a smaller version of "a hot Negro orchestra." As he had wanted to do as a young teen, Prima was now dancing to the sound he loved, and he was the one creating it with the best sidemen he'd ever had. He sang and blew his horn as he jumped and strutted around the stage, hot jive movements that no audience would see Benny Goodman or Guy Lombardo or any white bandleader do, but Cab Calloway would. As Mick Jagger would do thirty years later when the Rolling Stones burst on the scene, Louis Prima sang and moved like a black entertainer filled with the combined spirits of jazz, blues, and pop.

One woman in particular set her cap for Prima; she apparently adored him. But what intrigued him was that she had a lot of talent and was already far from just a face in the crowd. Martha Raye (born Margy Reed, from Butte, Montana) would later become known for musical comedy, and in her TV years in the 1960s and '70s she adopted the persona of a big-mouthed, brassy broad. But in the mid-1930s she was an aspiring actress and talented jazz singer. She became infatuated with the act at the Famous Door and attended dozens of shows.

"To me, Martha Raye was a great singer with a natural feel for improvisation," Arnold Shaw quoted Prima in *The Street That Never Slept.* "If she had stuck to singing, she would have been a great one."

As it was, she was stuck on Prima, who, like Raye, would also be criticized as his career progressed for choosing musical comedy over straight jazz. (They would also share the dubious distinction of having twelve spouses between them.) They were believed to be an item offstage, but what made the newspapers were the reports of their impromptu pairings on the Famous Door stage. When Louis spotted her at a table he introduced her to the audience, who demanded that she join the band.

While the Depression still held a grip on the United States, in New York City it was nonetheless a great time to be a musician, or at least a popular one. In 1919, when Prohibition began and many musicians had yet to emigrate north, there were four jazz clubs in New York. By the time Prima headlined at the Famous Door, there were thirty-five such clubs.

Yet, for the restless Prima, it was already time to go.

9

Prima and his band continued to record for the Brunswick label during their Famous Door engagement. In May 1935, when they cut a new version of "The Lady in Red," a highlight in addition to the dueling between Louis's trumpet and Pee Wee's clarinet was Prima's Armstrong inspired scat singing. Also recorded at the time were "Chinatown" and "Chasing Shadows." All three became hits that summer across the country, which, along with an appearance he and Kaye made on Rudy Vallee's national radio show, brought Louis Prima and His New Orleans Gang to the attention of people on the West Coast.

It might have seemed like too much of a career risk for Prima to leave New York. Jack Colt had given him raises to keep him at the Famous Door. The Brunswick sessions allowed him to record his own compositions as well as standards, and the records were selling. Walter Winchell and other newspaper columnists continued to write about him regularly. He was only twenty-four, and there was plenty of time to become an even bigger success in New York. But apparently, other than of mobsters, Prima had no fear. When he was approached about having a piece of a Famous Door nightclub in Los Angeles, he and his band packed their bags.

First there was a trip that had to be especially sweet for Prima—to New Orleans. When the train arrived that September, it signaled a triumphant return. In less than a year he had gone from local stardom to national recognition and being one of the biggest names in the Big Apple. With the now-named New Orleans Five, he performed for cheering crowds for five nights at the Shim Sham Club, at 229 Bourbon Street in the French Quarter, owned by his brother, Leon, who had also achieved success in New Orleans but apparently did not share his brother's grander ambitions. Prima's return was a jolt of good news for the city, which was in mourning over the assassination of Governor Huey Long only a few days earlier.

Jack Colt never had the same success at the Famous Door with another act. Billie Holiday, in her first show outside of Harlem clubs, was one of the performers who replaced Prima on that stage, and even she, with Teddy Wilson on piano, could not generate similar excitement. No doubt even worse for Holiday was the fact that she was not permitted to sit at a table or the bar, and so between sets she had to sit upstairs just outside the toilets. After four nights, she was fired.

Colt contacted Prima and offered another raise if he would come back to New York, but the bandleader was too intrigued by what Los Angeles had to offer. After filling up on Angelina's cooking and visiting with the family (spending very little time with Louise and Joyce), Louis got back on a train, this time heading west.

In Los Angeles, the Hollywood Famous Door opened on Vine Street. The nightclub swells had never seen an act like Louis Prima and the New Orleans Five, and they ate it up. Leon had tagged along to manage the band, and he was able to see the impact the boisterous show had on audiences. Also soon returning on guitar was Frank Federico, who became a Prima sideman for the next eleven years.

Word quickly got around that there was a new musical sheriff in town, and he was at the Hollywood Famous Door. "That club was filled every night with the biggest stars in the industry at that time," reported Joe Segreto in the 1999 documentary on Prima. "They all became Louis's very good friends. He played poker with Spencer Tracy and Walt Disney and all those guys. Certainly, he was excited to be out there."

And the women on the West Coast were excited about him being there too. There were plenty of starlets available, but according to some accounts, he became involved with one of the biggest stars in Hollywood.

"The last person who Jean Harlow loved was Louis," contended Gia Maione, Prima's widow, in *Louis Prima: The Wildest!*. "Her chauffeur would bring her to the Famous Door and she'd sit back in a smoky corner and watch Louis perform and wait for the show to be over to spend her time with Louis."

In 1932, when Harlow was only twenty-one, she appeared in *Red Dust*, a hit with Clark Gable. She became bigger at the box office with *China Seas*, *Hold Your Man*, and *Wife vs. Secretary* and was the top female star at MGM, which claimed to have "more stars than there are in the heavens."

In 1935, when she would have met Prima, she was ending her third marriage. It was also at this time she became involved with and was eventually engaged to William Powell, star of *The Thin Man* and other popular thrillers and comedies. If an affair with Prima took place, it would have been when Powell wasn't looking. In any case, she died in 1937 from kidney disease.

"I think Louis was very serious about Jean Harlow and she about him," Segreto said. "He was on a train when he saw a newspaper hit the ground, like the guys would throw a bundle on the ground, and there was a big headline about Harlow dying and I think he was quite saddened about that."

Thanks to Hollywood, Prima was reunited with a former flame. After doing a series of short, documentary-like films—one, titled *Swing It*, marked the film debut of Lucille Ball—Prima was incongruously cast as a cowboy in *Rhythm on the Range*, headlined by Bing Crosby and newcomers Martha Raye and Frances Farmer. Prima gamely backed up the two singers in what would seem to be an inauspicious start in the movie business, but fueled by the public's adulation of Crosby, the musical was a box-office hit. So was *Rose of Washington Square* with Tyrone Power, Al Jolson, and Alice Faye.

Prima appeared in several more movies—one of the more unusual casts had him mugging next to Gene Autry and new baseball star Joe DiMaggio— playing either himself or a fictional bandleader, so he never had reason to stretch much as an actor. None of the films was able to capture his roof-raising stage performances, even *Start Cheering* in 1938, which had him singing and hoofing alongside Jimmy Durante. Still, because of these appearances, he became better known to people around the country who were buying his records, not just those in New York and Los Angeles.

It was obvious that his marriage could survive neither the geographical distance nor the affairs. Early in 1936, Louise petitioned for a divorce in

New Orleans, and it was granted. Soon afterward Alma Ross, an aspiring actress from Minnesota, attended a show at the Hollywood Famous Door and caught Louis's eye.

Prima and Ross attended various Hollywood social events and night-clubs together and were mentioned as an item in the gossip columns. The relationship became very serious quickly. Oddly, Louis waited until he was on the road with his band to propose marriage. Alma met him in the Mid-west, and when they encountered Guy Lombardo in Chicago, he invited the couple to accompany him to a gig in South Bend, Indiana, where they could be married, with Lombardo as the best man.

When the newlyweds returned to Los Angeles, it seemed that Louis and Alma could become one of the more prominent couples in Tinseltown. She signed a seven-year contract with Paramount Pictures and played support-ing roles in several movies. He returned to the Hollywood Famous Door to play to packed houses. He started to form a larger band so he could join the more famous and higher-paid likes of Benny Goodman, Tommy Dorsey, and Lombardo as orchestra leaders.

In October 1936, he thought he was ready. The New Orleans Five had evolved into a twelve-piece group that still included Russell and Federico, and now had singer Velma Rae. For a sort of out-of-town tryout, he took the band to Chicago, where it debuted at the high-profile Blackhawk Club. It was a disastrous experience in front of a full house and plenty of press. The band just wasn't ready to play together as a cohesive unit, and it looked like the twenty-five-year-old leader had bitten off more than he could chew.

Prima couldn't get the problems with the disjointed band straightened out, and he eventually abandoned both the Blackhawk Club—the owners were not sorry to see him go—and, for several years, the big band format. Along the way he lost Pee Wee Russell, who felt uncomfortable playing in an orchestra, where there was less improvisation.

"I don't like big bands," Russell explained in a biography by Robert Hil-bert. "You are too regimented. Not that I mind being told what to do, but I can't bear to play that same note every night."

He decided to stay on in Chicago, and he and Prima never worked together again. Though plagued by alcoholism, Russell remained one of the great jazz clarinetists, and toward the end of his life (he died in 1969) he was still doing innovative work with a new generation of admiring musicians who included Gerry Mulligan and Thelonious Monk.

Back to leading a fast and furious five-piece band, Prima went in search of a fresh burst of popularity. He found it where he had found the first one: late in 1937, the band played at the original Famous Door in New York, and they were a smash all over again.

"Louis Prima, that trumpet-tooting madman, is currently delivering the high notes at his old alma mater," wrote nightlife columnist Theodore Strauss in the *New York Times*. "And on a street where the rhythms are notoriously fast and the music loud, Mr. Prima steps up the pace a notch or two. His trumpet playing, which took his breath away, took ours away too. He is the hottest man on the three stops we know. His band is small, not the usual fourteen-piece outfit crowding the tiny Fifty-second Street basements, but under Mr. Prima's leadership they go to town with a will, fast and in the groove. Racy stuff."

"I was glad to get back to Fifty-second Street," Prima later told reporters. "There was something about that street. I can't find the words. It always reminded me of old Bourbon Street in New Orleans. But it was more than just the music. It was a feeling that it gave you."

To Jack Colt's delight, they stayed for a record-breaking twenty weeks. They left in May 1938 only after being signed by the legendary producer Billy Rose to appear on a bill with the Three Stooges at the Casa Mañana theater, where they packed the house for seven weeks. (Prima and Moe Howard's paths would cross again twenty years later in Hollywood.)

But what is arguably Prima's greatest contribution to American music had been showcased that winter just a few blocks away in, of all places, Carnegie Hall.

10

———

Benny Goodman and Louis Prima had encountered each other in Hollywood as well as New York City, and at some point Goodman had added Prima's "Sing, Sing, Sing (With a Swing)" to his orchestra's repertoire. It was already a hit when Goodman was booked to play Carnegie Hall in January 1938. However, because of that performance, the song went from a popular hit to a jazz classic.

Goodman was born on May 30, 1909, in a poor section of Chicago, the ninth of twelve children. His ticket out of poverty was learning to play the clarinet, and playing it better than anyone else by the time he was a teenager—with, of course, the possible exception of Pee Wee Russell.

In 1934, at only twenty-five, he pulled together his first big band. Goodman was inspired by an orchestra led by Ben Pollack that was a big dance band incorporating some jazz onto its playlist. With the exception of the Casa Loma Orchestra and a band just begun by Jimmy and Tommy Dorsey (with arrangements by Glenn Miller), no white bandleaders devoted themselves exclusively to jazz, whereas white audiences embraced the sounds of groups led by Duke Ellington, Chick Webb, Jimmie Lunceford, Bennie Moten, and Fletcher Henderson.

Before the end of the year the Benny Goodman Orchestra was one of the three bands—the other two were led by Ken Murray and Xavier

Cugat—featured every Saturday night on "Let's Dance," a program broadcast nationally on NBC radio. Goodman was a brilliant bandleader as well as musician, one reason being that he recognized strong talent and material. Many of his up-tempo jazz arrangements were written by Fletcher Henderson, who juggled doing arrangements for others with leading his own band.

While Goodman did not invent swing music—he and many critics often referred to it as "sweet" music—he became the man most closely associated with it. Many critics have maintained that when the Benny Goodman Orchestra opened at the Palomar Ballroom in Los Angeles on August 21, 1935, to a rabidly enthusiastic crowd, the Swing Era began. Goodman rode the wave, urging his group to greater heights. In the 1936 *Downbeat* readers' popularity poll, the orchestra received three times as many votes as the second-place band.

Goodman pushed the envelope of jazz and with it American culture and society. When not leading his orchestra, he headed a trio that recorded and performed onstage together. When he hired Teddy Wilson to play piano, it was the first time (as far as most people knew) that the taboo against having a black musician appear onstage with a white group was broken. Later, the trio became a quartet with the addition of black vibraphonist Lionel Hampton. An oft-overlooked innovation by Goodman took place in 1939 when he invited Charlie Christian, another black musician, to play an electric guitar onstage, the first time an audience in New York saw that instrument.

After the Palomar triumph and with Henderson stretched thin, Goodman hired Jimmy Mundy as a full-time staff arranger. Mundy had been a member of a black band led by Earl Hines in Chicago but may have been eager to move on because their regular gig was at the Grand Terrace, a club frequented by John Dillinger, Pretty Boy Floyd, and the Capone brothers. *Killer-diller* was a term coined to describe the hard-charging arrangements that Mundy created.

Mundy saw that "Sing, Sing, Sing" was ripe for reinvention. The lyrics were simple:

> *Sing, sing, sing, sing*
> *Everybody start to sing*
> *Like dee dee dee bah bah bah dah*

Now you're singin' with a swing.
When the music goes around
Everybody goes to town
But here is one thing you should know
Sing, sing, sing, sing
Everybody starts to sing
Like dee dee dee bah bah bah dah
Now you're singin' with a swing.

There was already a foot-tapping melody. There was room for individual musicians to freelance. And a powerful orchestra like Goodman's could give the song a socko ending.

Prima composed the song in either late 1935 or early 1936, because it was first recorded by his New Orleans Five on February 28, 1936, in Los Angeles. According to what he later told his fifth wife, Gia, the song originated during his racetrack outings with Bing Crosby. Every time Crosby picked a horse in a race, for luck he'd sing its name, getting louder as the race went on. Prima urged him on by shouting, "Sing, Bing, sing!" That kept going through his head, and it evolved into the song "Sing, Sing, Sing." By the time his orchestra played it live at the Blackhawk in Chicago on October 11, 1936, it had replaced "Let's Have a Jubilee" as Prima's theme song.

As Goodman's group performed "Sing, Sing, Sing" more often in concert, it kept adding to the original "hot" arrangement. One night in particular at the end of the song, an especially inspired Gene Krupa didn't stop drumming, so Goodman resumed the clarinet, and the rest of "Sing, Sing, Sing" was improvised. According to Goodman biographer Ross Firestone, "By the time Benny recorded the expanded arrangement in 1937, it had grown to be over eight minutes long and covered both sides of a twelve-inch 78-RPM record." A version of the song can be heard and seen in the 1937 movie *Hollywood Hotel*.

Simply put, the reason the Benny Goodman Orchestra became the first jazz band to cross over to play Carnegie Hall—esteemed home to Arturo Toscanini and Leopold Stokowski and their orchestras, which played the works of Beethoven, Brahms, and Wagner—was to help promote cigarettes. The R. J. Reynolds Tobacco Company was looking for something new to feature on its *Camel Caravan* musical variety radio show. A publicist at the firm handling the Camel account suggested Goodman's band. Initially, Goodman refused because he felt Carnegie Hall was too conservative a venue for the hot jazz he played exclusively now and tanking there would attract more attention than an unsuccessful performance at another venue. But upon further reflection, Goodman accepted the challenge. Succeeding at Carnegie Hall, he reasoned, would be a huge boost for jazz.

"It was a great winter for swing music in New York," wrote Firestone. "Tommy Dorsey was playing across town at the Palm Room of the Commodore Hotel. After two years on the Coast his brother Jimmy returned east and replaced the Casa Loma at the New Yorker. Cab Calloway was at the Cotton Club. Mezz Mezzrow's short-lived all-star mixed orchestra played a brief engagement at the Harlem Uproar House. Chick Webb was still taking on all comers at the Savoy. Louis Prima and Art Tatum were holding forth at the Famous Door. In January Count Basie went into the Loew's State on Broadway."

Impresario Sol Hurok set aside January 16, a Sunday night, for the concert. Ticket prices ranged from eighty cents to $2.75. Goodman would not make a nickel on this gig, but if he was able to win over what might be a tough crowd to the side of swing music, that would be worth more than money. In a fortuitous bit of timing, on January 12, *Hollywood Hotel*, the musical featuring the Benny Goodman Orchestra, opened at the Strand Theater in New York and became an immediate hit.

Carnegie Hall sold out, all 2,760 seats, and another hundred chairs that had been set up were sold too. A line formed that afternoon for standing-room tickets. By 8:45, when the show began, not another person could be shoehorned into the place.

"Don't Be That Way" was the first number, followed by "Sometimes I'm Happy," "One O'Clock Jump," "I'm Coming Virginia," "When My Baby Smiles at Me," and "Shine," which featured Harry James paying homage to Louis Armstrong's solo on the 1931 recording. Three members of Duke Ellington's orchestra—all African American, of course—joined Goodman's group to perform Ellington's "Blue Reverie." After another song, Count Basie, Lester Young, and three other members of the Count's band came out onstage for a free-flowing jam session. Obviously, Goodman was also using the concert at Carnegie Hall as an opportunity to further break the unwritten ban on black and white musicians appearing together.

With Teddy Wilson on piano and Gene Krupa on drums, Goodman's trio performed "Body and Soul." Then Lionel Hampton came out, and the quartet did "Avalon," "The Man I Love," and "I Got Rhythm." The audience was in a frenzy, which was a good time for an intermission because there was plenty of music left to play.

The second half of the concert opened with "Blue Skies" followed by a swing version of the Scottish song "Loch Lomond," and then "Blue Room" and "Swingtime in the Rockies." With the crowd shouting and trying to dance in their seats, Goodman abandoned the program and brought out Wilson and Hampton again for numbers by the trio and quartet. Then the entire orchestra returned, and everyone in the hall braced for the grand finale.

Krupa banged away on the tom-tom to launch "Sing, Sing, Sing." After several minutes of inspired solos and driving ensemble work there was silence, and, thinking the song was over, the audience began applauding. But in the tradition of "you ain't seen nothin' yet," a tenor saxophone resumed the tune; Krupa performed another solo as did Harry James on trumpet. Then it was Goodman's turn for a clarinet solo that sounded like a pure stream of consciousness. That was followed by an almost contemplative two-minute piano solo. It concluded with Krupa bashing the cowbells and the band racing to a rousing climax. The entire performance lasted over twelve minutes and left the audience exhausted.

Oddly, the critics of the day were ambivalent about the obviously popular success of the Carnegie Hall show. The opinions of those who attended and heard about it on the jazz grapevine easily won out over the years. *The Famous 1938 Carnegie Hall Jazz Concert* was finally issued in 1950 and "became one of the best-selling jazz albums of all time," according to Firestone, "and the night of January 16 came to be enshrined as the absolute pinnacle of Benny's career and one of the truly important landmarks in the whole history of jazz."

Over the years Goodman would often be referred to as the King of Swing. A big reason for that was the collective memory of "Sing, Sing, Sing" performed by the Benny Goodman Orchestra being one of the watershed moments in American music. To this day there are people surprised to find that Louis Prima, not Goodman, composed it, though in fairness the version performed by Goodman's band elevated the song to the status of music legend.

What did that Carnegie Hall concert mean for Prima's career? It validated him as a composer within jazz music circles. A big feather in his cap was that Benny Goodman, the most popular bandleader in the United States (and probably beyond), had chosen the Prima song as a climax to his concerts. And it sure didn't hurt that he would receive residuals for an enduring classic, though not as much recognition as Goodman.

11

———

When Louis Prima and his band made their highly publicized comeback in New York and the performance of "Sing, Sing, Sing (With a Swing)" had audiences swooning in their seats, Dorothy Jacqueline Keely was just short of ten years old. She was born to Howard Keely, a carpenter, and Fanny Stevens on March 9, 1928, in Norfolk, Virginia. (Throughout most of her career, however, her birth year was given as 1932.) The closest Dot, as she was called, came to having musical surroundings was her mother playing the organ in church.

Her parents divorced when she was nine. When her mother remarried, Dot took on the last name of her new stepfather, Jesse Smith, also a carpenter. Dot's biological father was half-Cherokee and half-Irish, and her grandmother was a full-blooded Cherokee. Dot was the only daughter out of four children. (Unlike their sister, the brothers would retain their childhood nicknames for the rest of their lives—Dumps, Piggy, and Buster.) The family of six took in laundry to help make ends meet.

"We lived in a very bad section of Norfolk called Atlantic City," Smith remembered. "When I say bad, I mean every thief, every hooker, every anybody that did anything bad that landed in jail came from this little section of town that I lived in."

For whatever reason, Dot liked to sing. She performed at social gatherings.

One time her mother found her "sleep-singing": though asleep, she was standing on her bed doing the Ink Spots' "I Don't Want to Set the World on Fire."

At age eleven, Dot Smith agreed to accompany a friend, Rae Robinson, to a local radio studio, where Rae planned to audition for "Joe Brown's Radio Gang," a popular regional program and act. Brown asked Dot if she also sang, and she replied, "Yes, but just for my family." Brown persuaded her to warble something, and she sang "White Lies and Red Roses." When she was done, Dot, not her friend, got the job. Instead of being paid, however, she paid a dollar a week after that to learn new songs.

"Joe Brown's Radio Gang" performed on Friday and Saturday nights at venues in and around Norfolk. The emerging Dot Smith learned to please an audience as well as how to sing a wide range of songs. At fourteen, during World War II, she sang at a bond rally at her high school, and in the audience was Saxie Dowell, who led a band at the Norfolk Naval Aid Station. He had played saxophone for Glenn Miller, Tommy Dorsey, and other big-band leaders in the 1930s, but his main claim to fame was composing "Three Little Fishes," a hit song for Kay Kyser.

This bond rally stint performance resulted in Dowell hiring Dot. Her mother was glad for the few dollars this gig brought in but was not pleased at how her teenaged daughter was openly ogled by the sailors while onstage and when she sang off the back of a truck driven around Norfolk. Offstage, and when not in school, Dot listened to the radio, and her favorite singers were June Christy and Ella Fitzgerald.

It was a step up when bandleader Earl Bennett hired Dot, paying her five dollars a night for performances. This enabled Dot to buy clothes and books for school. Because Dot was underage, her mother accompanied her to the nightclubs where the band played.

During the summer of 1947, Dot and her family went on a vacation to New York, but because of the heat they took a detour to Atlantic City in New Jersey. Two of her brothers liked to jitterbug and wanted to go to the Steel Pier, where many big bands performed. They saw a large banner advertising "Louis Prima and His Orchestra," and a big crowd surrounded the bandstand. She picked up her youngest brother (born to Fanny and Jesse) to help get through the crowd. Prima was in the middle of his show, and Dot was enthralled.

According to Smith, she was not familiar with Prima at that time. "The band was so good and so funny. I edged my way up to the stage and placed my little brother on it, and I stood there absolutely mesmerized watching this man. I just stood there dumbfounded. I had never seen anything like it before. Besides being one of the best bands to dance to, they were funny. The comedy was unbelievable."

One brother pointed at Prima and told her that the bandleader kept staring at her. "I must have had a look he liked," Smith said. "He never said a word to me, though, the whole day."

She went home and listened to Louis's music nonstop, learning his arrangements. If the Prima band ever came to the Norfolk area, she would be ready to imagine that she was part of it.

12

Despite the success of his New Orleans Five in New York and the embarrassment of his Chicago orchestra outing—and perhaps goaded by Goodman's success with the song he had composed—Prima wanted to try the big band format again. This made sense in that the big bands dominated the dance halls and record charts in the years immediately before World War II. There was ego involved, too—he wanted to be as famous as Goodman, Ellington, and the Dorsey Brothers. He was certainly more of a showman than they were, so it was a matter of blending his personal jump, jive, and wail style with a crisp orchestra that would supply the balance and the basic dance grooves. But to do so he would have to set aside the kind of music that had brought him to where he now stood.

"The big band era of the 1930s and '40s pretty much wiped out the whole New Orleans approach to jazz," says Bruce Raeburn of the Hogan Jazz Archive. "The small combo, doing collective improvisation, all of this was taken over though some of it got featured in big bands. The music was pretty much organized by arrangers and band leaders. By 1940, Louis Prima had a big band which he called the Gleeby Rhythm Orchestra, which was a great name, and you can see what he's doing over the course of the early 1940s. He was appealing to the public. He was trying to find the sound that they wanted."

The orchestra Prima put together—which he sometimes also dubbed the "Be Happy" Orchestra—would eventually contain as many as eighteen musicians. They spent most of their time in cars on the road. The Gleeby Rhythm Orchestra could play in Kansas City one night, St. Louis the next night, and Cincinnati the night after that. It was indeed one of the most popular acts in the country. When Prima wasn't on the road he could be found in a recording studio, producing the orchestra's latest records.

He and Guy Lombardo were among the "name bands" that headlined the 1939 World's Fair in New York. For the Prima show that August, three thousand seats were set up "with room for many more thousands to stand near by," the *New York Times* reported.

With the attack on Pearl Harbor on December 7, 1941, Prima's thirty-first birthday, the United States entered World War II. The war had no effect on his popularity, but Prima from time to time had to replace musicians who enlisted or were drafted, and gas rationing forced the William Morris Agency to arrange for more geographically prudent bookings for the band. Prima spent more time in the Northeast, with the occasional foray to New Orleans or Miami Beach.

Depleted ranks didn't cause him much concern because ultimately the entire act was on his shoulders. "Louis Prima, in an eight-week run at the Syracuse Hotel, has brought the spot the biggest business of the season," *Billboard* reported in 1942. "Prima, fronting with his torrid trumpet, now has a commercial band that does both hot and sweet numbers and Prima is still the showman of old."

"Louis Prima and his orchestra enjoy top-billing in this week's vaudeville entertainment at Loew's State Theatre," reported the *New York Times* on March 19, 1943. "Other performers on the program include Jackie Green, comic; the Debonettes, dancers, and Carlton Emmy and the Mad Wags, dog act."

Unlike the less ethnic big bands, a good portion of the Prima repertoire consisted of familiar Italian tunes, such as "Josephina," "Please No Squeeza Da Banana," and "Bacciagaloop, Makes Love on the Stoop," and music he wrote himself. One song was dedicated to his mother, "Angelina." (The presumption has always been that this song was written by Prima as a tribute to his mother, but in fact it was composed by Doris Fisher, who was also known for another novelty hit, "Tutti-Frutti.") While this fare was a big reason why jazz critics wrote negatively, sometimes scathingly, about the Gleeby Rhythm Orchestra, such songs were real crowd-pleasers.

A more cautious and less confident bandleader would have ditched these tunes during World War II because Italy was a member of the Axis. But Prima knew his audience, and his popularity actually increased.

"When Mussolini joined Hitler, all of the Italians were sort of, how would I say, dumbfounded, because they didn't think it would happen, so maybe you stay away from that music," said Leon Prima. "But Louis stayed with the Italian trend, he still played the Italian music and used the Italian words."

"Obviously, one of the things that made Louis Prima very special and different from other trumpet players and singers was the Italian element," said Will Friedwald in *Louis Prima: The Wildest!*. "It's not just the fact that it's Italian, but that it's any type of ethnicity group, because there really wasn't one; there was no big star at that point who stressed his ethnic group." It is not a stretch to say that because the popular Prima exhibited such pride in his heritage, audiences remained more open to a new generation of Italian singers who emerged during and after the war, among them Perry Como, Tony Bennett, Dean Martin, and Vic Damone.

During the war, Prima's orchestra was one of only three white groups to perform at the Apollo Theater in Harlem, and they did so seven times in four years, compared to twice each for the other bands. They also appeared at the Royal Theatre in Baltimore, the Howard Theatre in Washington, D.C., the Regal in Chicago, the Paradise in Detroit, and other venues where the performers and most of the audiences traditionally were black. Prima shrewdly included in the band's lineup songs with a local connection or references to please the hometown audience, such as "Boogie in Chicago" and "Brooklyn Boogie" (which he cowrote), and when he played black venues he always sang, with a sly grin, "It Takes a Long, Tall, Brown-Skin Gal."

With Ellington, Calloway, Armstrong, Fletcher Henderson, and Count Basie so popular, it was not unusual for black artists to cross over and play for and have their records purchased by a white audience, but Prima more than any other white bandleader ensured it was not exclusively a one-way street. Sammy Davis Jr. once remarked that "half the people thought that Louis was black anyway, mixed. So he was a big favorite."

When not working, Prima had two favorite pursuits: women and horses. And he shared a problem with Ernest Hemingway: as F. Scott Fitzgerald once said, "The problem isn't that Ernest keeps falling in love, it's that he marries all of them."

Even Keely Smith later admitted, "Louis could have any woman he wanted." The most enthusiastic members of his audience were female. The Louis Prima Fan Club consisted of forty thousand acolytes—thirty-five thousand of them women, who dubbed themselves the Prima Donnas.

His devotion to horse racing would eventually cost him a lot of money, but he made some along the way too. It wasn't enough that he went to the track, he had to also own racehorses. In front of 28,430 spectators at a New York racetrack in 1944, a five-year-old gelding he owned, Play Pretty, was a surprise winner and paid $9.10.

But most of Prima's seemingly limitless energy was devoted to music. Like Goodman, he had the knack for recognizing talent. (And like Goodman, he put on integrated performances, also working with Wilson and Hampton.) He preferred to have a regular lineup of good musicians, and he worked them hard in rehearsals so that what they did onstage would sound flawless while appearing spontaneous.

Jimmy Vincent once recalled that he played with the Prima orchestra for a month, and then one night Prima asked the audience to vote on whether the drummer should become officially part of the band. "I was with him for twenty-four years," said Vincent in *Louis Prima: The Wildest!*.

He also recalled: "Every time we worked in a theater, during the rehearsal all the light men from the front and the side would come down and say, 'Let us give you the rundown of the show.' Louis said, 'We don't need no rundown.' 'What are you talking about?' Louis told them, 'I'll direct you with my hands. Just follow me.' Louis liked to work with his hands. So as the show goes on, he's going here, there, pinpointing here, you over there, lights off, a little meeker, doing this the whole time, and he's got them where they're grooving now, everybody in the place. He did that every theater we worked in, directing with his hands always."

When the orchestra played New Orleans—such as a very successful run at the St. Charles Theatre in 1944—Louis took as many members as could fit to the house on St. Peter Street to feast on Angelina's cooking.

"When Louis would come home, the kitchen and dining room and living room were all opened up to the musicians," Madeline Prima remembered. "We didn't get to eat up there until Louis was gone."

"It was a day for red gravy," said Joe Segreto. "The meal would open with meatballs with the gravy, and we would have the pasta, and copious wonderful meals, and the family all around you and the friends of the family made it an exciting day."

Vincent remembered a conversation with Mrs. Prima: "She's doing the dishes, and I'm talking some Italian, and we're grooving, and Louis is in the living room reading, and he's listening to us. 'Where do you think Louis got that talent?' Angelina says. 'From me. From me, Jimmy.' 'What do you mean?' 'I used to be the singer in church.' 'You did? What did you do?' 'I was the singer.' 'How do you sing?' And she starts in. I'm slapping out a beat and Louis is hysterical."

In the audience at one of Prima's shows in Washington, D.C., in early 1944 was First Lady Eleanor Roosevelt. She apparently could not resist the bandleader's charms either, and she invited him to the White House.

A number of celebrities, including actresses Joan Fontaine and Mary Pickford, had been invited for a gathering to celebrate President Franklin Roosevelt's sixty-second birthday. Prima joined them. The grandson of Sicilian immigrants from Little Palermo in New Orleans stood in the East Room of the White House with various government officials and then was introduced to the president. The hyped-up Prima blurted, "Hello, Daddy!" Fortunately, Roosevelt thought this was hilarious. When a group portrait was taken, Prima stood next to Mrs. Roosevelt, and thus his fame was further boosted when the photo was published in newspapers across the country.

By the end of World War II, at age thirty-four Louis Prima was in the top tier of successful American entertainers. At a show in New York City in 1945, he shared the stage with Frank Sinatra. The predominantly female audience swooned and cheered more for Prima whenever he sang or blew the trumpet.

The problem, as he found out, was that from here there was nowhere to go but down.

13

___

After the war, the musical tastes of audiences in the United States began to change. As a result, big bands faded in popularity. For bandleaders like Prima, as concert revenues dwindled, it became more difficult to bankroll the larger groups of musicians. Some bands went out of business altogether, while others struggled on or downsized, becoming quintets or even quartets.

Prima pushed ahead with the latest incarnation of the Gleeby Rhythm Orchestra. He continued to record—he signed a new contract with RCA Victor Records—and he remained popular. A six-week engagement in 1945 at the Strand Theatre in New York grossed $440,000, and in 1946 *Metronome* magazine recognized him as Showman of the Year. But his spending continued at a high level, not just to underwrite his band but also to buy and maintain racehorses. Having two ex-wives didn't help either.

Louis was not a faithful husband while on the road, and his traveling so much put a strain on his marriage to Alma. Finally, in 1947, she sued him for divorce. It was granted, along with alimony of 7.5 percent of his annual income. (Eleven years later, the terms were changed to a forty-five-thousand-dollar payment and $250 a week.) He began dating Tracelene Barrett, who had once been his secretary and was all of twenty-one.

In June 1948, the two were married in New York City. Angelina and Anthony Prima attended, with the former singing during the reception.

The couple launched their honeymoon by getting on a boat that Louis had bought for his bride and named the *Tracelene II*. In what could be seen as symbolic, the boat hit a sandbar in the middle of the Hudson River, and the newlyweds had to be rescued.

Prima spent less time on the road, apparently, to please his new wife and not to curtail expenses, as in addition to the boat he rented an apartment in the city and bought property just outside New Orleans that became known as Pretty Acres. He continued to own and bet on the ponies, and he purchased a majority interest in a New Orleans nightclub. His musicians began to leave him to pursue other opportunities. More people were staying home and hooking up televisions, but Louis wanted nothing to do with that medium. In 1949, Tracelene gave birth to Louis's second daughter, also named Tracelene.

He had a big hit in 1947 with "Civilization," and the story behind it shows Prima's good ear for a tune. Carl Sigman and Bob Hilliard were writing songs for the orchestra at the Copacabana in New York, but "Civilization" was rejected as being kind of silly for the swells who made up the Copa crowd. ("Bongo bongo bongo, I don't want to leave the Congo" is a typical lyric.) The composers then put it in a Broadway revue, *Angel in the Wings*, where it was sung by Elaine Stritch, a dynamic singer making her Broadway debut.

Prima heard about the song and secured the rights to record it right away, and it lingered in the Top 10 for eight weeks. When Sigman showed up at Prima's office in the Brill Building with more song candidates, he fell in love with the secretary whose job responsibilities included signing photos of Louis for fans, taking dictation, and placing his bets on horses. They later married, costing Prima a valuable assistant.

As a composer, Prima continued to craft a good tune, as shown when he cowrote "A Sunday Kind of Love," which was a hit for Jo Stafford and Fran Warren. It was reported that in 1948 he earned half a million dollars from residuals, performances, his piece of the New Orleans nightclub, and other interests.

But that was his peak as a big-band leader and composer. Those bands were falling out of fashion, and the high overhead of the salaries and the traveling made them especially vulnerable. More of the audience were now fans of the singers who had emerged to front the musicians, like Sinatra and Doris Day and Perry Como.

"The crunch came in 1947," wrote Cab Calloway in his memoir. "Movies were in, small combos were in, bebop was in, and big bands were out. I just couldn't get the bookings for the big band, so I called the band members together." He told them, "I've got to let most of you go. The big bands may come back, but right now it's not happening."

In the summer of 1948, Dot Smith was twenty, though she could easily pass for younger. She still lived with her family, still doing some singing, and she worked a day job as a bookkeeper. She had been pestering the owner of the Surf Club in Virginia Beach to book Louis Prima and his band. Finally, he did, for that August.

In the weeks leading up to the show, Dot worked on packing the place as though she were the promoter. According to a Prima recollection, when he and his sidemen drove into the area, he saw a young woman in a dark swimsuit emerging from the water. He couldn't take his eyes off her, and he vaguely remembered the girl in the audience at the Steel Pier who had caught his eye the year before. This might seem far-fetched given the number of women who made up Prima's audiences night after night, week after week, but by all accounts he did have an uncanny eye for women, one that matched his appetite for them.

During the first show at the Surf Club that Friday night, Prima announced that he was looking for a new singer. Lily Ann Carol had left for a solo career, and replacements Florida Keyes and Tangerine hadn't cut the mustard. Several local girls tried out, but Dot, too nervous and shy, did not. There were more auditions on Saturday, again without Dot participating, and Prima still didn't find what he was looking for.

The band performed at an afternoon tea dance on Sunday. Having attended the past two nights and with it being a hot summer day, during the show Dot was at the beach outside the club. Suddenly, she heard an announcement from inside the club: "Dot Smith, come to the bandstand."

She was alarmed, thinking that something had happened to a family member. She rushed into the Surf Club, after borrowing a skirt and a blouse to get in. Jimmy Vincent recalled, "We're playing in Virginia and there's a beautiful nightclub, and oh, she was right in front of us."

"Louis was standing there, and I said did you call my name?" Smith related in *Louis Prima: The Wildest!*. "And he said, 'Yes, I understand that you're a singer.' And I said yes. And he said, 'I want you to come up and sing a couple of songs.' Well, I started shaking like you can't believe. My knees wouldn't stop knocking and I was barefoot, but I sang. And he hired me right then and there and I went to work with him that night on the spot and left with him the following Thursday."

Dot, already knowing the arrangements, sang "Embraceable You" and "Sleepy Time Gal." During that night's show she performed in her only dress, the one she had worn to her high school prom.

On their way out of town—on the band's travels until Dot turned twenty-one in March 1949, Dot's mother and her brother Piggy would alternate as chaperones—Louis urged that she change her name. His suggestion was Dottie Mae. Dot insisted, "I'm no Dottie Mae." Instead, combining her two real last names, she became Keely Smith.

Thus one of the most innovative and successful male and female partnerships in show business history began.

When the band returned to Virginia Beach the following summer, Prima wanted to give the audience something to remember him by in exchange for having taken a local girl away. To end the show, Prima led the playing and singing band off the stage of the Surf Club and right into the Atlantic Ocean.

ACT II

That Old Black Magic

14

———

Keely Smith turned out to be exactly what Louis Prima needed to put him back on top in show business. He was smart enough to recognize her potential. First, there was her large, natural voice. Keely could sing high and low, fast and slow, and her smooth phrasing was enticing, especially in contrast to his braying bellow. (Alluring too was her Virginia "Ah" substituting for "I" in songs.) During her peak years, some critics would say that if you looked up *sultry* in the dictionary, there would be a photo of Keely Smith. It wouldn't matter that she couldn't read music; she was a natural with a strong memory. Her appealing Irish-Cherokee looks kept audiences' eyes on her.

In the ensuing years, Prima's instincts told him to emphasize Keely's physical features, especially her face, by presenting her with a pageboy haircut and encouraging a deadpan look that conveyed an attitude that she didn't care what was going on around her. At least, Louis took all the credit for these stagings.

But Smith's bored appearance was not a Prima invention. She was truly bored onstage. "It wasn't a role," she explained. "It was something that I did, I was never a hand-clapper or a finger-snapper."

Because most of the stages they played on were small, Keely had to stand in the background until it was time for her to sing, and her wait could be a while as Louis sang and blew his trumpet and danced around. "I used to just cross my arms across my chest and for a half-hour I just stood there and did nothing," Keely said. She watched the audience and people getting up and sitting down, "and I was so busy doing what I call being nosy that when Louis would come and shake my skirt and do motions to me, I would look at him like, 'You're interrupting my train of thought.' It gave the impression that I was deadpan and that I was angry with him."

Another time she explained, "I stood there like a dummy. That was no act. That's bashful. Louis wouldn't let anyone change me."

Louis, always the best at reading an audience, saw how people reacted to Keely's stage persona and made sure it remained part of the act for years afterward. It was up to Prima to grab her attention, and he would try just about anything to win at least a smile from her. The more she managed to resist his jokes and ad-libs, the harder he tried. When he did get a reaction—sometimes Keely couldn't help bursting out with laughter—he and by extension the audience were especially pleased.

One of Keely's most distinctive features was her pageboy haircut, and most accounts have attributed this to Louis's insistence. But, according to Keely, "When I joined Louis on the road, we were playing venues similar to the Surf Club, but also the black theaters on the East Coast and big ballrooms all over the country. But none of them had air-conditioning. One night onstage, I was unbearably hot and I noticed a girl in the audience with a cute bobbed hairstyle. During the half-time, I went backstage, and she cut off my long hair."

She added, "When Louis saw it, he wanted to kill me. But it worked out good."

What really made the developing Louis and Keely collaboration work was that, for the first time in Louis's life, equally important to him as his music was his attraction to his stage partner. His relationship with his first wife, Louise, remained strictly offstage. She shared little of his professional career, and their marriage ended relatively quickly. Alma was in the entertainment business but not necessarily in music, and she wasn't nearly as ambitious as Louis was. Tracelene had been his secretary and not involved in creative pursuits.

For Louis, Keely combined work and play. Within her was a large reservoir of untapped talent. On top of that, he became infatuated with her, emotionally and physically. Barbara Belle, Louis's manager and occasional songwriting partner through 1961, told Garry Boulard in a 1986 interview that Louis had joked that, when he first saw Dot Smith in a bikini, he "knew she had to be a good singer."

Though Louis was eighteen years older, for Keely the feeling was mutual. "I thought he was the most gorgeous thing that ever walked," Keely said. "He could look at me with his eyes and he could just melt me completely—no matter what he had done."

What became an intense love story did not happen overnight, however. In the ensuing years, Smith recalled several times that Prima was "too hairy," and she was put off by his apelike features, which was how Louis was often portrayed in caricatures and reviews of the act. Another time, to the *San Francisco Chronicle*, she said, "I didn't like him at first, but he sure grew on me."

Leaving Virginia Beach behind, Keely gave no indication that she thought that she was hitching her wagon to a guy who would lead her to a glamorous show-business lifestyle complete with all the fame and baubles that went with it. She would always maintain that she was sort of swept away by Louis and that going on the road with him and his band was an exciting opportunity.

In reality, far from landing on Easy Street, Keely was in for a bumpy ride. While Prima's career could never be said to be in freefall, it was slipping. He still made money thanks to the songs he composed, some longtime fans still showed up at concerts, and there were those who were curious about his new girl singer. But as time went on, the shows were more spaced apart, with diminishing crowds, and in smaller venues. Supporting a band and a stable of horses on the ninety-seven-acre Pretty Acres estate in Louisiana was becoming more of a drain on his wallet.

"They cost Louis a lot of money," Keely told Garry Boulard about the racehorses. "We were doing one-nighters everywhere just to support Louis's horses. We'd go 700 to 800 miles to do a one-nighter, pick up something like seven hundred dollars, and then hit the road again—all for the horses."

Prima wanted to keep "playing pretty for the people," as he liked to say, but there were now fewer people, and they were farther apart.

Stubbornly, he kept looking for them. "We traveled on the bus, and Louis rode in a Cadillac," recalls Michael Dastoli, who played saxophone in

Prima's band in the late 1940s. "We traveled all over the Midwest during the summertime playing the fairs, then in the wintertime we were booked three nights at a theater in Boston, then a week at a place in Rhode Island, and we even tried Canada. Wherever we could get a booking, we went.

"We used to come across Harry James and his band traveling by bus, and Tommy Dorsey too," Dastoli continues. "Louis was a nut for softball, so when we were in Atlantic City for a week and Count Basie or one of the other bands was there, we'd play as many games as we could. Of course, Louis had to be the pitcher."

However large or small the crowd, Prima still gave them a show. Dastoli remembers that Prima "wasn't the kind of guy you could get close to," and that he kept to himself offstage, but "what he used to do onstage was fantastic. He was a great showman. He wouldn't warm up; he was always ready. Louis would come onstage and blow one note, and off we went."

Dastoli wanted to remain with Prima's band indefinitely, as he enjoyed the good times on the road and the music. But he had begun dating a woman who had come to see the band in Atlantic City. One day, Dastoli said, "She gave me an ultimatum as we were driving: go on to the church and make our plans to get married, or she's not going to see me anymore." Dastoli and his wife, Josephine, have been married for over sixty years.

As with wives, Prima could not maintain a steady relationship with a record label. He and Keely recorded together as early as 1949, but they didn't stick with any one label, waxing songs for RCA, Mercury, Robin Hood, Columbia, and Decca in rapid succession.

One indication of his changing fortunes was that in December 1950 when *Mr. Music*, the latest Bing Crosby vehicle—it also featured Nancy Olson, Charles Coburn, Peggy Lee, and Groucho Marx—opened at the Paramount Theater in New York, headlining the stage show was Louis Prima and his orchestra. Two years later, when the Bob Hope, Jane Russell, and Roy Rogers oater *Son of Paleface* opened at the Paramount, Prima and his band were listed as the last of three acts, behind the Five DeMarco Sisters and Los Gatos.

In between, in September 1951, "Louis Prima and his Orchestra featuring Keely Smith," as the act was billed, was booked into the Paramount, but not as the headliner. That honor went to a twenty-five-year-old who had scored two hit records that summer, "Because of You" and "Cold, Cold Heart."

"The greatest thing about that gig was getting the chance to work with Louis Prima, another of my show business heroes," Tony Bennett remembered in *The Good Life*. "He was terrific. Prima was a genius of a showman, a wild man on stage that you just couldn't take your eyes off . . . by the time I got on stage the crowd was wide awake and on the edge of their seats. They're all thinking, 'What's going to happen now? How can anybody follow what we just saw?'"

Prima did some whistling past the graveyard, telling reporters that he was contemplating retirement and would devote himself to his horses and playing golf. (Several years earlier he had announced that he was retiring to become a treasure hunter in the Florida Keys, but that had been strictly a publicity stunt.) He would wait out this drought, and when the big band sound made a comeback, he would be ready.

But Prima could be stubborn for only so long, especially with alimony and child support to pay. He had to lose the orchestra and go back to basics. It was like starting out all over again.

"[Prima] was near to hitting professional bottom," wrote James Ritz, a jazz historian, about the singer's situation. "He was a 43-year-old has-been with few prospects on the books."

"If the big band thing wasn't going to work, go back to the formula that worked for him earlier in New York," said Joe Segreto in *Louis Prima: The Wildest!*.

"He really didn't want to let the big band go," said Keely. "It's when the big bands couldn't be supported any longer, he had no choice. For a long time, we worked just him and I, and we would work with little groups and really dump clubs in upstate New York, every anywhere that we could find work."

Keely told Garry Boulard in 1986, "We started to work the dumps, really. Things got bad rather quickly. We worked at all sorts of Godawful places. And we'd go in and work with whatever house band was available—two pieces, three pieces, six pieces, whatever. Just the two of us."

Recalling those difficult years in a 1958 interview with the *Los Angeles Times*, Keely said, "In those days Louis had plenty of *delusioni*. Know what it means? Means aggravations in Italian. So we decided to get married—and Louis lost his *delusioni*."

In a scenario reminiscent of the hit 1937 movie *A Star Is Born*, with Fredric March as the fading leading man and young Janet Gaynor as the newcomer about to break through, Keely didn't let Louis's declining fame and earning power prevent her from being in love with him and staying committed to him and his music. She still had a whole career ahead of her, while he had already burned through two or three.

Where was Tracelene in all this? For a short time she had continued to travel with Louis and the band, often with Keely in the car with them. The birth of her daughter put her on the sidelines and spared her the humiliation of watching her husband grow fonder of her replacement as he spent less time at home and more time on the road, which was a financial necessity.

The attraction between Louis and Keely was clear to all, and no doubt Tracelene received reports of this. She accepted pretty gracefully that she had become history. She divorced Louis on June 18, 1953, with her residence by that time being Volusia County, Florida. She was awarded seventy-five dollars a week in child support. The paltry amount that he could afford may well have embarrassed Prima more than being a three-time loser in marriage. It also indicated how low his income had fallen since his previous divorce.

He and Keely were married where they had officially first met, in Virginia Beach, on July 13, 1953. Audiences and any press that bothered to report the news were led to believe that she was now twenty-one when in fact she was twenty-five, and Louis was forty-two. The greater age disparity was better for the act of aging lothario trying to appeal to the virginal ingénue.

And Louis designed their act to appeal to a younger audience. He was beginning to hear and read in the trade papers about the music that would be called rock 'n' roll. He already knew plenty about swing, jazz, and the Dixieland of his native New Orleans. He incorporated all of these when he wrote and arranged songs. In addition, as he and Keely got closer and she acquired more stage experience, the rapport between them was obvious—his clowning and her sort of resisting him until he won her over was a novelty.

People loved them together—but still not enough people. For another year they continued to play to small audiences in dismal, cheap clubs. This allowed them to further develop the dynamic of their act, but playing backwater towns did not get them into the spotlight that Prima, especially, craved. He began to pay attention to items in newspapers about Las Vegas.

"He was one of the first people to realize the potential of Las Vegas," says Bruce Raeburn.

"Louis finally put a call in to the Sahara Hotel to a very good friend of his named Bill Miller," Keely recalled. "This was the same Bill Miller from the Riviera in New Jersey that was a big nightclub back there. Louis told him the truth. He said, 'Bill, we're on our rear, and we need a job.' Bill didn't know who I was, naturally. He said, 'Bill, I think I'm going to go home and put together a small group like I used to have in New York. What do you think about that?' And Bill told him, 'Hey Louis, I don't have anything.' And Louis called him a few times, and finally he gave us two weeks in November." Opening night was to be the twenty-fourth—six days later.

They were living in a small apartment in New York City. There was no time to go to New Orleans. Louis and Keely and five musicians jumped into cars and headed west. This last gasp to keep his career afloat had to work— Louis was about to become a father again.

"Being pregnant, I got sick all along the way—it felt like in every state— and with each stop our caravan came to a halt," Keely remembered in the foreword to *Fabulous Las Vegas in the '50s*, published in 1999.

But the caravan pushed on, needing to reach the Sahara.

15

———

Bill Miller was the entertainment director of the Sahara Hotel in the fall of 1954. It had opened on October 7, 1952, and was dubbed the Jewel of the Desert by Milton Prell, the principal owner. (The term *owner* was used loosely in Las Vegas because most of the money and power behind the large hotels came from the mob.) It had a whopping 276 rooms and was the sixth major hotel to be built on the Strip. Its Middle East theme was easily apparent thanks to the two huge statues of camels that bookended the entrance.

When Miller told Prima that he "didn't have anything," he meant there were no open dates in the hotel's main showroom, where well-known stars performed regularly. With some reluctance, because he thought he was insulting Prima, Miller offered the two weeks in the Casbar Lounge, essentially a side room that fit only 150 people. It contained a bar, and it was where people went for a drink and a smoke between bouts of gambling. There was no cover or minimum. Entertainment—actually, *good* entertainment—could be a disadvantage, because if people lingered in the lounge, they were spending less time losing money at the gaming tables.

The last time Prima had performed in Las Vegas was pre-Keely, and he had been the headliner at the El Rancho. Now he was given the favor of trying to entertain drunks and people who were focused on that next rush of adrenaline from the clanging slot machines and clicking roulette wheels.

"We had no lights to speak of, just a little thing you stepped under, a tiny spotlight," Keely wrote about the couple's first look at the lounge. "The sound was one microphone and whatever speakers they had in the room. No monitors either. There was really no sound of any kind."

It has often been reported—incorrectly—that the Prima-Smith act began the tradition of having live music in a Las Vegas hotel lounge. They made it nationally popular, but the Strip already had very good acts established in lounge settings—such as Freddie Bell and his Bellboys, and especially the Mary Kaye Trio.

That group had first formed in St. Louis as the Mary Kaaihue Trio, reflecting her Hawaiian heritage. With her brother Norman and comedian Frank Ross, the renamed trio made its debut in Las Vegas in the Horn Room of the Last Frontier Hotel in 1947. Their spontaneous, freewheeling style attracted bigger crowds, and by the time Louis and Keely arrived, the Mary Kaye Trio had played to appreciative audiences at several lounges along the Strip, including in the Sahara.

In the Casbar Lounge, people sat at tables drinking and smoking and re-energizing for their next round of gambling. Until acts like the Mary Kaye Trio and Louis Prima and Keely Smith came along, the stigma was that you played the lounge because you weren't enough of a headliner to attract an audience to fill the main showroom. As Miller had intimated, for many other performers the lounge was a venue for those on the way down, not the way up.

A lot of entertainers would have balked at making the trip to Las Vegas from New York for a two-week gig in a lounge—to practically end up playing for free—but Prima knew that he had no choice but to roll the dice and hope for some good reviews that could lead to better offers. He and Keely were living hand-to-mouth by this point (even the horses had been sold off), so any payday was welcome. And yet, even with the stakes so high, Louis almost blew the opportunity.

When he and Keely arrived in Las Vegas, they went to the Sahara Hotel to scope out the lounge. Keeping the Casbar warm that night was Cab Calloway. His fortunes had picked up a bit because of playing the role of Sportin' Life in the 1950 Broadway revival of *Porgy and Bess*, which was appropriate because, according to Calloway, "George Gershwin used to spend a lot of time in the Cotton Club during the thirties and the characterization of Sportin' Life was drawn directly from my performances. In fact, in 1935, when *Porgy* was first produced, I was asked to play the part of Sportin' Life but I turned it down because I was too busy with the band and the club." However, as a live musical act in Las Vegas, he was just another struggling ex–big-band leader hoping to hang on.

Louis knew Cab from Apollo Theatre and Cotton Club days, and when his Sahara show was over, Calloway came to sit with Louis and Keely and have a drink. Prima was astonished to be informed that blacks were not allowed to sit at the tables in the Casbar Lounge.

According to Keely's recollection, her husband "went into a rage and wanted to quit right then. We were both deeply offended, but thank goodness Bill Miller was unavailable somewhere in Mexico, and we were forced to open."

However, before that could happen, they had to rehearse and figure out what would work in the close confines of the lounge. And let people know that they were in town. Though he had been down on his luck, Louis figured his name still meant something. He took out quarter-page display ads in the *Las Vegas Review-Journal* and the *Las Vegas Sun* announcing "Louis Prima and His All-Star Quintet" at the Hotel Sahara. This was at a time when it was unusual for a lounge act to advertise.

The musicians Louis and Keely brought with them had shared some of their travels and travails. The act opened and they were good—not great, but good enough that Miller, still seeing how desperate Louis was, offered him the opportunity to continue in the lounge the week after Christmas. It wasn't the most promising gig, but Louis took it.

"We opened in Las Vegas on November 24, 1954," recalled Keely. "We went there with a two-week contract, and we stayed six years."

But that was after something important that had been missing in the act those first two weeks was injected. After six years of performing together, Louis and Keely had formed a strong stage, as well as personal, collaboration. But they weren't getting all they needed from the band.

According to Joe Segreto, "Louis went to his brother in New Orleans. Leon had a fabulous young saxophone player playing at his place who had gained some renown down there known as Sam Butera."

Butera had been born on August 17, 1927. His father owned the Poor Boy's Grocery & Meat Market in a black section of the city, and in his spare time Joe Butera Sr. played the concertina and guitar. Sam saw a saxophone played for the first time at a wedding when he was seven, and he was immediately smitten. Though he learned the clarinet too, he was devoted to being a sax player. It could be said that at the age of fourteen he became a professional because he began serving as a sort of human jukebox for stripper clubs on Bourbon Street. "I worked every joint on that street," Butera told an interviewer. "You name it and I worked it. All those girls wanted to do was mother me." He rebounded—or progressed from—that experience at eighteen to win a contest at Carnegie Hall and was profiled in a *Look* magazine feature on the top young jazz players in the United States.

Sam couldn't finish high school soon enough, and when he did he was hired to play in a band headed by Ray McKinley. By this time his major influences were Charlie Parker, Lester Young, Gene Ammons, and Lee Allen, who occasionally invited the young saxman to play with a band headed by Paul Gayten, one of his father's meat-market customers. Sam had made his recording debut on McKinley's versions of "Celery Stalks at Midnight" and a recent national hit, "Civilization," which would continue to get mileage years after Prima's version.

Butera formed his own band, and they began an engagement at the 500 Club, owned by Leon Prima. He was on the lookout for a recording contract, and his break came after a featured spot in a concert with Woody Herman's band. Butera made several records for the RCA and Groove labels. He went on the road with DJ Alan Freed's first rock 'n' roll tour of the East Coast, giving him some exposure beyond New Orleans, and he spent time playing in Tommy Dorsey's band.

Bebop jazz was the style that Butera cared for most, but he found it hard to get gigs in the New Orleans area playing that way. By the time he first encountered Prima, who was back in New Orleans (perhaps for a preholiday family get-together after the initial Sahara gig), Butera had been listening to the records of rock 'n' roll pioneers—including Fats Domino, also of New Orleans—and borrowing some of their beat and combining it with some of the honking sax sounds bleating out of clubs in the French Quarter.

"When I met Louis, I had a job at a place right on the highway outside of New Orleans," recalled Butera about Perez's Oasis Club in Metairie, where he led a band called the Night Trainers, in 1954. "Leon had said to him, 'This kid does a lot of business, Louis. Let him play with your band.' Louis said sure. So I went on the stage and I get a couple of songs with his band. After I got through, Louis said, 'Sam, I'm going to Vegas, if anything happens I'm going to call you.' I said, 'Gee, wonderful. How much money?' 'Don't worry about it,' Louis said."

Very soon after, Louis called Sam and said, "You better come out here, and bring a few other guys." He wanted Butera there on Christmas Day itself, but the sax player, perhaps not realizing how close he was cutting it, insisted that he be home on Christmas with his wife, Vera, and their children and that instead he would get there on the twenty-sixth.

That was opening night of the new act in the Casbar Lounge. As they were getting ready for the curtain to open, Sam tried unsuccessfully to introduce the sidemen to Louis and Keely. During the show, when Louis asked Sam who they were, he shouted "The Witnesses!" That is what Butera's band would remain for their run in Las Vegas and beyond.

"I have to be honest and say this: until Sam came, the group didn't really cook," Keely said. "They were nice guys, and they were pretty good musicians, but Sam was the front that Louis needed to work off of."

"He came up with the idea of using a blend of rock 'n' roll rhythm, a blend of rhythm and blues, and that which he had always done, which was a kind of a shuffle beat," Will Friedwald said in the documentary *Louis Prima: The Wildest!*.

It wasn't just Butera's musicianship and active stage presence that made Prima's band different from any other. He started writing arrangements for the Witnesses in a shuffle beat that pushed the 4/4 rhythm onto the snare drum and made the song feel twice as fast as it really was. What emerged was a distinctive Witnesses sound that other bands would try to imitate without much success.

"[Butera] brought to their stage show a driving sound and a flair for showmanship that perfectly complemented Prima's," wrote music critic Joseph F. Laredo. "It was a musical partnership made in heaven."

Suddenly, everything clicked. According to Keely, "Louis and I had worked hard for years to create a good act, but it was when Sam and the boys showed up that we knew we had something special."

People literally left the slot machines and gaming tables to check out the wild sound in the lounge. That was OK, because within just a few nights the act was bringing more people into the Sahara than ever before, creating a bigger reservoir of gamblers in the place. "We didn't just play music—we put on a show," Keely wrote in *Fabulous Las Vegas in the '50s*. "Little by little, the crowds started getting so big the room had to be enclosed. Drapes were put up, which helped muffle the sound because we were loud, louder than the pit bosses, dice tables and the slot machines."

Miller cleared the schedule so that Prima and his act could play the lounge indefinitely. The *Las Vegas Sun* raved that Louis and Keely were "absolutely the hottest combo to hit this town yet" and that they were destined to be the "all-time record holders for Las Vegas lounges," which, at that time, wasn't the highest praise possible.

The band that Sam had pulled together in December consisted of Jimmy "Little Red" Blount on trombone, Jack Marshall on guitar, Willie McComber Jr. on keyboards, Bobby Morris on drums, and Amado Rodrigues on bass. This lineup would change—often because Louis was considered too much the penny-pincher—but still the band would become tighter over the years. Even as 1955 began, it had already brought to Las Vegas an original, thrilling sound.

The act was a smash. Word went along the Strip fast that there was something new and different and . . . well, "wild" going on at the Sahara Hotel. The *Review-Journal* reported under a photograph of Louis: "Exclusive Columbia recording artist Louis Prima and his all star quintet not only make records but they break records. Prima's extended stay in the Casbar Lounge has been the high point of Las Vegas' musical entertainment. Louis features his pretty wife, Keely Smith, in comedy and special arrangements. Their appearance has made the Casbar the entertainment hub of our fun center."

Louis Prima and Keely Smith and the Witnesses did five shows a night and dripped with sweat when they left the lounge not long before the winter dawn. Bill Miller's problem was no longer where to find room to fit the act in but to find more and more weeks to keep the act going.

The timing for Louis and Keely couldn't have been better. Fewer than nine thousand people lived in Las Vegas during World War II. By 1954, there were over forty-five thousand, and it was the fastest-growing small city in the country. In those days gossip about celebrities didn't stay in Vegas; it instead filled up the pages of newspapers and magazines around the country. People would find out about a hot "new" act real soon.

In addition to the music, what made the band hot was the dynamic between the aggressive and virile Louis and . . . well, Keely could no longer play the virginal ingénue as her belly grew bigger, but she was still the female figure to be wooed and won over. They appeared to be more deeply in love than ever. There did not seem to be any pretense about it. Louis was not one then or later to talk about their emotional life, but Keely repeatedly reported on how much in love she was with her husband. Miraculously, on his fourth try, Louis had hit matrimonial pay dirt. Many people in the audience lived vicariously through this idealized relationship. It was indeed a love story, and every night that the act knocked 'em dead reinforced the expectation that Louis and Keely would live happily ever after.

While the rapport between Louis and Keely was not new, just intensified, working with Sam Butera and his handpicked sidemen and the vein-popping, toe-tapping sound they all produced together was. According to jazz critic Scott Shea: "The banter between Louis and Keely was not without its share of innuendo and off-color references. Surrounding the jokes and the gags, and keeping everything jumping, were Butera and the Witnesses, supplying a wild, relentless, driving beat that punched through the lounge's smoke and chatter and left crowds in awe. There was nothing like it."

"I remember working with Louis in Brooklyn when his singer was Lily Carol and he was on his way to becoming a small-time band, especially after Lily left and married a friend of mine who was a sax player," recalls comedian Jack Carter. "Then he comes to Vegas with Keely Smith and the impact was tremendous. People were elbowing each other out of the way to get in."

And Prima's well-honed stage personality and catalogue were new to the Nevada audience who flocked to the growing neon city to have fun. "Louis Prima had the most exclusively humorous slant of all trumpeters," wrote Friedwald in *Jazz Singing*. "By the time he had made it to Las Vegas especially, he had worked out the details on a performance method completely devoted to breaking people up, as funny in its own way as Victor Borge or Spike Jones. Prima brought to banal novelties the same dedication of purpose that Toscanini brought to Verdi or that Leonard Bernstein brought to the Broadway musical, and 'Hitsum Kitsum Bumpity Itsum' means just as much to Prima as 'Body and Soul' does to Coleman Hawkins. His wonderfully flaunted irreverence, as when he 'outlines' (feeds the lyrics of) the Neopolitan pop song 'Oh Marie' ('Maria Mari') in *Italian* for a chorus of Mitch Miller–inspired WASPs, has such an absolute purity to it that it becomes incredibly reverent."

According to Garry Boulard's analysis, "What Prima's interest in rock 'n' roll displayed was his desire to find a musical style not only complementary to Keely, but also different enough to firmly etch her in the public's mind as unique. Prima had an idea about music in the 1950s: The best sound, he decided, would be one that mixed aspects of Dixieland, jazz, swing, and rock 'n' roll. This was a revolutionary thought in the business. In 1954 the lines between such styles were firmly drawn with musicians rarely venturing to cross such borders, much less combine elements of each genre. But Prima had freely mixed musical influences in his songs throughout his career, and suffered the hostile reviews of critics less imaginative than he for it."

What was also new to Louis and Keely's performance was that every day her due date approached. The pregnancy didn't affect the act too much, because for much of the time Keely remained rooted to one spot anyway, but she felt increasingly tired.

She probably would have enjoyed going to the movies, if she'd had time for it. In the third week in December a most popular film was, of course, *White Christmas* starring Bing Crosby, Danny Kaye, Rosemary Clooney, and Vera-Ellen. It replaced *Reap the Wild Wind* with John Wayne and Paulette Goddard at the El Portal theater. More rugged fare available was *Yellow Mountain* with Lex Barker and Howard Duff ("They battled for the golden heart of a fabulous mountain . . . and a woman's unclaimed lips!") at the Palace, and down the street was the double feature of *Drum Beat* with Alan Ladd and *Return to Treasure Island* with Tab Hunter. Coming attractions were being shown for *Black Widow* with Ginger Rogers, Van Heflin, and George Raft, *Track of the Cat* starring future Keely costar Robert Mitchum and Teresa Wright, and *Abbott and Costello Meet the Keystone Kops*.

An indication that the Primas' quick success allowed them to be embraced by people who mattered in Las Vegas was this item in the January 8, 1955, edition of the weekly publication *Fabulous Las Vegas*: "We think it was a very fine gesture for Debbie and Milton Prell (owners of the Hotel Sahara) to toss a Stork Party for Mrs. Louis Prima, professionally known as Keely Smith. The gathering was held at the Prells' lovely home January 5th and the attendance rivaled the Casbar supporters. The Primas expect their image in March. The expectant mother is still performing on stage and spectators still can't believe her blessed event is due so shortly."

At first, the word of mouth was that Louis, Keely, and Sam were doing the "wildest show in town." Soon, however, the "official" nickname for the act became "The Wildest."

16

Next to New Orleans, Las Vegas was the most accommodating home that Louis Prima would ever have. And of all places, the city and its surroundings had a good number of Italians even before the mob moved in. The first Italian immigrants arrived in Nevada in the 1860s to toil as miners in the Comstock Lode. They invested their wages in land throughout the state, and some became ranchers while others established businesses in small settlements.

The first non-Indian to set foot in the Las Vegas Valley was Rafael Rivera. He was a scout in a sixty-man party led by Antonio Armijo, a Mexican trader, along the Spanish Trail to Los Angeles in 1829. On Christmas Day they camped a hundred miles northeast of what is today Las Vegas, and Rivera went in search of water. He discovered the Las Vegas Springs. Travel routes were changed so that people going to and from Los Angeles could stop and drink from the Springs.

Las Vegas itself was actually first settled by Mormons from Utah who built a mission in 1855, when the area was part of Arizona, to provide protection for the Los Angeles–Salt Lake City mail route. The first mention of Las Vegas had been eleven years earlier, when explorer John C. Fremont camped near the desert springs and recorded the name, which meant "The Meadows." The place, then part of territory that still belonged to Mexico, began to appear on Spanish maps.

Why was a settlement founded at Las Vegas as opposed to other sites in southwestern Nevada? (The state was created and admitted to the Union in 1864 as the "Battle Born State.") The same element that has such a profound impact on the city today: water. There were natural underground springs that when tapped made the Las Vegas Valley livable.

Beset by difficulties that included intense heat and Indian raids, the Mormons left after only three years, and their mission land became part of an expanding ranch owned by Octavius Gass. Archibald Stewart bought the land in 1881, and after he was murdered three years later, his wife ran the two-thousand-acre Las Vegas Rancho until 1902, when it was purchased by the San Pedro, Los Angeles, and Salt Lake Railroad—founded by the crooked Senator William Clark of Montana—because of the available water.

Las Vegas was established on May 15, 1905, essentially as a railroad town, with the depot at Fremont and Main Streets. The city was incorporated six years later. The town's residents were mostly laborers, and the station was the main stop between Los Angeles and Salt Lake City. Its ice plant, the only one between Salt Lake City and San Bernardino, allowed produce to be shipped across the desert. The two primary sections of Las Vegas were its downtown business area and its red-light district. The Hotel Nevada, built in 1906, was the place to stay for people passing through, and the following year the first telephone in Las Vegas was installed in the hotel and electric lights first glowed on Fremont Street. A movie theater opened in 1928. Ironically, the first feature shown was a Clara Bow movie titled *Ladies of the Mob*.

Everything changed in 1931 when the Nevada divorce laws were loosened and gambling became legal in the state. Immediately after the legislature acted, a casino featuring gaming and entertainment was opened by Tony Cornero, who made little attempt to hide his Cosa Nostra connections. Another Italian American, Frank Detra, opened the Pair-O-Dice (the club was purchased from a former Los Angeles vice squad captain), and a third, Pietro Silvagni, opened the Hotel Apache to accommodate those coming from out of town to gamble. Another significant event in 1931 was the beginning of construction of the Boulder (later Hoover) Dam thirty miles to the south. This project brought thousands more people to the area during the decade. "Helldorado Day" was first held in 1935 and evolved into a four-day festival celebration targeted specifically at entertaining the tourists and attracting more of them to the city.

Las Vegas truly began to grow during the 1940s because of World War II and the mob's increasing interest. A military base nearby enticed workers who rented and then bought inexpensive housing and began families there. In 1941, the El Rancho Vegas hotel and casino was built on Highway 91. It was a beachhead on the four-mile stretch of highway within the city that would become known as the Strip. That same year, the El Cortez Hotel opened in the downtown area.

Because of his flamboyant reputation and, decades later, the film directed by and starring Warren Beatty, Bugsy Siegel has received most of the attention for creating Las Vegas as a gambling hot spot in the 1940s. The gangster did play a pivotal role, but his Flamingo casino was only one of four resort hotels built on the Strip during the decade.

By the time he was eighteen, in 1923, Siegel had an extensive criminal record in New York as a member of the notorious crime organization Murder Incorporated. By his late twenties, even he had forgotten how many people he had murdered. When Prohibition ended, it was time to send him west, to take over the horse-racing wire and other gambling operations in Los Angeles on behalf of Meyer Lansky, one of the most powerful gang bosses in the country, who had a paternal fondness for the young sociopath.

Siegel was wildly successful. It was estimated that by the late 1930s he was overseeing a five-hundred-thousand-dollar-a-day bookmaking operation. In addition to that, Lansky, with Siegel's assistance, grossed a billion dollars a year on heroin sales in the United States. There was so much money, it became necessary to find a new outlet to launder and stash some of it while sending the rest to overseas accounts. Siegel was dispatched to check out Las Vegas. He liked what he saw, and reported that to his boss.

With an investment of $245,000, the El Cortez, the first major downtown resort, was built in 1941. Within four years, among its owners were Siegel and Lansky, who liked to say, "The only man who wins in a casino is the man who owns the place."

Bugsy Siegel wanted to own his own place, or at least be at the top of the ownership heap. In November 1945, at a dinner at actor George Raft's house in Los Angeles, Siegel put together a consortium of people, including

Lansky, who would put up one million dollars to build the Flamingo Hotel in Las Vegas. With 195 shares total in the new Nevada Projects Corporation, Siegel had seventy more shares than the next-largest owner.

The goal was to open the Flamingo, on thirty acres with one thousand feet of frontage on the Strip, by or on Christmas Day 1946. Del Webb, who was also owner with Dan Topping of the New York Yankees, was to build it. Building materials were hard to come by so soon after the war, but Senator Pat McCarran took care of redirecting material coming into his home state to the Flamingo project, which sometimes meant that houses for returning war veterans had to be delayed. (The Las Vegas airport is named after McCarran.)

The project fell way behind, and costs kept escalating. One estimate was put at $6.5 million, which included money that Siegel's girlfriend, Virginia Hill—one of ten children from a backwoods Alabama family, she had turned tricks at the Chicago World's Fair as a teenager—was skimming off the top and depositing into a secret bank account. Still, Siegel insisted that it open on December 26, and it did. Jimmy Durante played to only about eighty guests, some of whom had to be put up at the El Rancho and Last Frontier hotels because the Flamingo wasn't finished. The weather was uncharacteristically wet, most of the Hollywood celebs stayed away, and the incomplete hotel impressed no one. During the next two months, as work on the rooms continued, hundreds of thousands of dollars more were lost.

Siegel's partners, despite a push for continued patience by Lansky, finally lost that patience with the delays, mismanagement, money losses, and the suspected skimming by Siegel and Hill. While sitting in the living room of Hill's home in Los Angeles on June 20, 1947, Siegel was shot twice in the head and twice in the chest by a .30-caliber Army carbine through a window. (His left eye was shot out, and the intact eyelid was found ten feet away.) Only five people showed up at his funeral. No one was arrested for the shooting, but the killers were known to be connected to Jack Ruby, the mobster who sixteen years later would murder John F. Kennedy's assassin, Lee Harvey Oswald.

Under new management, the Flamingo became successful and showcased the next generation of hotel-casinos establishing themselves on the Strip.

Las Vegas has the distinction of being the largest city in the United States incorporated in the twentieth century. This is pretty remarkable when one considers that much of its growth came after the century was almost half over. In 1950, the city's population was 24,624, three times what it was when the 1940s began.

Still, it was in the 1950s that Las Vegas truly took off as a vacation destination. Resort hotels couldn't be built fast enough along the Strip, with each one more spectacular—and, it seemed, with more neon signage—than the last one. By the end of the decade, the city's population had jumped to 64,405.

"The spectacular development of the Las Vegas Strip was the paramount story of the 1950s," wrote Eugene P. Moehring in *Resort City in the Sunbelt*. "As early as 1948, it was obvious that the highway south of Las Vegas would need more than four resorts to handle the growing waves of Californians driving to and from the city. Only the undeveloped tracts south of town possessed the space for parking lots, tennis courts, swimming pools, riding stables, and the other amenities which resort guests had increasingly come to expect. The crowded downtown lots bordering Fremont Street simply lacked the room to compete with their suburban counterparts south of town. The 1950s witnessed a hotel-building fever which eventually made Las Vegas famous."

Ironically, a big boost to Las Vegas had been the hearings held around the country by the Senate Committee on Organized Crime in Interstate Commerce, chaired by Estes Kefauver. In 1950 and '51, it traveled fifty-two thousand miles to fourteen cities taking testimony from over six hundred people. One outcome was the closing of casinos across the country that housed illegal gambling. Las Vegas, with its legal gaming, became even more of an oasis in the law-enforcement desert.

As if gambling weren't enough of a lure, the casino managers (who fronted for their mobster owners) booked entertainers into their main rooms. Such performers as Sophie Tucker (El Rancho Vegas), Rudy Vallee, Mickey Rooney (New Frontier), Jimmy Durante (Desert Inn), Eddie Cantor, and Maurice Chevalier (Dunes), whose Hollywood heydays were long over, found new life for their careers thanks to their name recognition and acts that featured beautiful showgirls. A steady stream of cars wheezed their way through the Mojave Desert from Los Angeles to Vegas, carrying current

Hollywood stars as well as blue-collar couples spending their weekends and some of the extra cash they earned in the economic boom of the 1950s.

According to Tony Bennett, who made his Las Vegas debut at the El Rancho in April 1952, "Those were sensational days. Entertainers like myself, Dean Martin, Frank Sinatra, Sammy Davis, Lena Horne, Count Basie, Duke Ellington, Noel Coward, Marlene Dietrich, Harpo Marx, and Louis Prima really made that town happen."

And, if the entertainment and gambling weren't appealing enough, there were the nuclear special effects. The U.S. government created the Nevada Test Site seventy miles northwest of Las Vegas in 1951, and city officials were happy to promote the clearly visible mushroom clouds as tourist attractions. Stylists at some of the hotels created hairdos that resembled mushroom clouds, restaurant menus featured "atomic burgers," and bartenders mixed champagne, vodka, and brandy to make "atomic cocktails." In less than four years, three dozen nuclear bombs were exploded at the site, and over a hundred by the end of the decade. There were reports that horses stopped eating and pets refused to be touched in the days following atomic tests, but there seemed to be little attention paid to the effect on the humans in the city or even the ones who had been allowed to drive out to the test sites to observe.

Las Vegas officials thought there was further promotional value in the B-grade movies that were made using the atomic explosions as a backdrop or plot device. *The Atomic Kid* was a comedy starring Mickey Rooney about a young man who gains unusual powers (such as glowing in the dark) after being exposed to one of the desert blasts. The script was written by Blake Edwards, who would go on to make such much-improved pictures as the Pink Panther series and *Days of Wine and Roses*. In 1957, three years after *The Atomic Kid* made only a small dent in the box office, *The Amazing Colossal Man*, which tells the tall tale of "a savage giant running amok in Las Vegas," was released. He does indeed wreak havoc along the Strip before Army firepower sends him plunging to the bottom of the Boulder Dam.

At the beginning of the decade, Moe Dalitz funneled mob money into the construction of the Desert Inn. "Vegas Vic," a huge neon cowboy, was fastened to the Pioneer Club in 1951 to welcome visitors. The two-story, 276-room Sahara Hotel, featuring Ray Bolger as the opening act, made its debut in December 1952. "The hotel was an immediate success; in fact, business was brisk enough that first year to justify construction of 200 more rooms in 1953," wrote Moehring. "Throughout the 1950s the resort was a hangout for stars and gamblers alike. John Wayne and Fred MacMurray frequently came and, even until his death, Elvis Presley (while he never headlined the Congo Room) often played the slots late into the night."

Also in December 1952, the Sands opened. The owner of the Desert Inn, Wilbur Clark, hosted the first nationally televised Tournament of Champions, allowing people around the nation to see Bing Crosby and Bob Hope and other celebrities jousting on the golf course, further enhancing Las Vegas's reputation as a playground.

There were still some Old West touches that clashed with the city's growth and path to urbanization. "Humane Society dog catchers were ordered today to make a wholesale roundup of scores of 'wild dogs' reportedly roaming Las Vegas subdivisions and raising havoc with new laws, milkmen and postal employees," began the lead story in the December 16, 1954, edition of the *Las Vegas Review-Journal*.

And the reading public enjoyed the occasional tawdry scandal. Sharing the same page in the *Review-Journal* was this lede: "Pat Bryant, 41, a pretty strip hotel waitress, whose looks belie her age, came into justice court for a preliminary hearing on charges of involuntary manslaughter growing out of the fatal shooting here last August of George Updaw, local casino dealer. The woman is charged with firing a bullet through a door and into the chest of Updaw. She said she had been locked out of Updaw's former wife's home, 2200 Santa Rita Dr., without her clothes."

The combination of anticipation of huge profits from gambling and an expanding drug empire—much of it under Lansky's supervision—led to an explosion of casino construction in Las Vegas on and near the Strip. Kefauver had definitely been onto something, but he just couldn't do anything about it, and even some of his colleagues in Congress were enjoying sojourns in the desert. With more mob money, the Showboat was built in 1954, featuring a five-hundred-seat Bingo room and a twenty-four-lane bowling alley. At year's end, tabulations showed that the city had attracted eight million visitors.

In April 1955, it was the Royal Nevada's turn to open its doors. That same month, the Riviera made its debut. With 320 rooms in nine stories, it was the first high-rise on the Strip—and thus featured the first elevators in a Strip hotel—and it also boasted a television set in every guestroom. The opening act was Liberace, and jaws dropped among the other hotel owners when it was revealed that he was being paid fifty thousand dollars a week. Also that year, the New Frontier was christened.

In May, the Dunes Hotel added to the glut of casinos that opened in 1955. It struggled financially until a new owner offered "Minsky's Follies," the first topless revue in Las Vegas. (In December 1957, the Dunes offered "Holiday for 'G' Strings," produced by Minsky.) When the Moulin Rouge opened that same May (a co-owner and host was the former heavyweight champion Joe Louis), Las Vegas had its first interracial hotel and casino, though it was on Bonanza Road, not the Strip. That edition of the Moulin Rouge lasted six months, crippled by financial troubles.

The competition for tourist dollars became as hot as the desert air in the second half of the decade. The Hacienda Hotel arrived on the Strip in June 1956. Ten months later came the opening of the Tropicana, and in October 1957 the Sans Souci opened across the street from the Sands. When the Stardust made its debut in July 1958, an attraction was a 27-feet-high, 217-feet-across sign that was the largest neon sign in the world and could be seen from three miles away. Also in 1958, construction began on the Las Vegas Convention Center, with its ninety-thousand-square-foot exhibit hall and main auditorium shaped like a flying saucer.

As Louis Prima and Keely Smith and Sam Butera and the Witnesses settled in at the Sahara in 1955 for what became a long run, a city of lights and stars grew around them. Louis's luck and timing allowed them to be right at the center of an entertainment scene that would change and to some extent dominate American culture for almost a decade.

17

"The success generated by Louis and the excitement was part of what created all of that whole entertainment furor in Las Vegas where every club and every casino had a fabulous show," said Joe Segreto in the documentary *Louis Prima: The Wildest!.* "He opened the door for all of that to happen."

According to James Ritz, "Visitors to Las Vegas latched onto Prima's show like a desperate gambler glomming a lucky streak. Soon Louis, Keely and Sam were the toast of the Strip, admittance to their shows in greater demand than that of some of the headliners in the main rooms."

In a Sahara print ad in January 1955, only a little over a month after the band came to town, "Louis Prima and His All-Star Quintet" received the top billing among four acts. Already Louis expected no less. He now had with him the best band since the Famous Door days in New York, and in Keely, his most talented singer, who was madly in love with him to boot. Yet he made sure that the band worked at getting better.

"Everything sounded spontaneous but we were well rehearsed," Butera said. "With Louis's laughter and Keely's presence and great singing, the group always looked like we were having fun. And we were, really."

"With Keely, the more she deadpanned, the funnier she was," says Jack Carter. "She stood there, and people roared and screamed. But when she sang, she had one of the best voices in the business. With that funny haircut and all, she stared at Louis like he was an idiot and people couldn't stop laughing."

It is interesting to note that, even with the acclaim Keely would receive over the years as a singer, she didn't necessarily view herself that way. "I'm actually nothing more than a clown," she told Wally George of the *Los Angeles Times* in an interview. "I'm a comic—that's why I complement Louis." Then she added: "You know how it is, like a man and his dog."

"They might not even have known it themselves, but Louis and Keely were more than ready to be a smash when they came to Las Vegas," says Lorraine Hunt-Bono, who before being elected lieutenant governor of Nevada in 1999 grew up in Las Vegas and was a casino and nightclub performer. "They had spent years doing the little clubs whether it was Lake George or Atlantic City or their home towns. They worked, they went to school with each other, and they had the chance to hone their craft. So when they came to Las Vegas, they were real pros. They had paid a lot of dues, but to us here they were new and fresh and very exciting."

Hunt-Bono was a teenager at the time and would not normally have been allowed in the Casbar Lounge, but she had a cousin who was a maitre d' there. He installed her in the back with a night's worth of soda, and she was enthralled.

"Louis was a master, an absolute master of leading the band, and of reading the audience, and he appeared to always know what to do to entertain the crowd," she says. "I watched and learned how he worked the audience. And how he revolved around Keely, whose character he had created. She was not going to jump around with dramatic gestures like all the other girl singers; she was supposed to stand there and every so often look at him like he was a bad, bad boy. Maybe that doesn't sound like much on her part, but Keely was a brilliant performer."

The success of the show re-energized Prima. He had turned forty-four in December 1954, which was not old for a performer even during the days when men's life expectancy was in their sixties. However, there was a lot of mileage on Louis. He had been driving audiences to distraction since playing on street corners in New Orleans. He had already packed several careers into one lifetime. He had a fourth wife who was only twenty-six. He made that disparity part of the act: in a performance of "Can't Help Loving That

Man" recorded live at the Sahara, Keely tells the audience, "I'm too young for this man," and Louis quickly chimes in, "That's a stage joke." She retorts, laughing, "I wish it was."

He had gotten another shot at the limelight and was going to make the most of it. And there was a competitive aspect. Keely was not necessarily seeking audience adulation—indeed, her stage persona projected that she couldn't care less—but she received it in increasing doses. Sam was simply knocking fellow musicians out with his saxophone and impressing still others—the Witnesses were the best backup band on the Strip. But the Chief, as Louis insisted on being called—not only to acknowledge who was the leader of the act but to further define his domineering relationship with his wife of Native American descent—was not about to be left behind.

A telling photo taken by John Bryson sometime during a night at the Casbar Lounge was distributed to the press. Keely stands center stage, surrounded by the drummer, bass player, and pianist, in a dark-shaded blouse and a wide white skirt adorned with a large flower. With her hands joined behind her back, she gazes impassively at a spot in the middle of the lounge. In that spot is Louis, lying on the floor blowing his trumpet with his legs bicycling. Bent over and blowing their saxophone and trombone at him are Sam and "Little Red" Blount. They are surrounded by patrons at small white tables who are laughing and smoking and looking a little like they are observing the inmates taking over the asylum and believing that is a wonderful thing.

It also helped that, according to Keely, once the act was established, "Louis changed everything. They had the service station for the bar right in front of the little stage. And a girl would walk up and say 'Three beers' and 'Two of this and two of that' while I'm in the middle of singing 'The Man I Love' or something. Louis got that moved to the far end of the bar. And we got a maitre d' who would seat people. It really turned out to be a nice lounge."

A sure sign that the act had made it in Las Vegas was that when performers were done with their shows, they came to the Casbar Lounge (also advertised as the Casbar Theater). Yes, it was more than convenient that Louis and Keely and the Witnesses still had hours to go when other acts were finishing at one or two in the morning, but they did come to see what

"The Wildest" was really about, and with good reason. It became even more difficult for Keely to maintain her deadpan look as she gazed out at the tables and saw some of the most famous entertainers in the world sitting at some of them.

"Everybody was there," said Butera. "Every star, when they got through work, there wasn't a seat in the lounge. This is no baloney. It's true."

Segreto said, "Sinatra would go with Sammy Davis and those guys and say, 'Look what this guy is doing. Look what he's creating here. That's what we have to create. Look what excitement he's causing.'"

"You look anywhere around the lounge and there was a star," Butera added. "There's a star, and another star, and there was another star. You couldn't acknowledge everybody."

"Louis always found a way to break things up, and also to get people to come up onstage," Jack Carter remembers. "We'd always get up with him and do a number, because we all knew every song, everybody did. The other performers certainly did. That was a big thing in the act, that these terrific performers would be up onstage. It didn't matter if it was the one o'clock show or the three o'clock, that lounge was packed."

The SRO crowds meant that Louis was putting money back in his pockets, and he and his wife began to think that this Las Vegas gig could last a while and maybe they should think about staying put even after Keely had the baby. They were living in an apartment on Malroney Street and wanted to be in a better part of town, especially after a thief broke in and tossed the place, taking $235 in cash and Keely's watch.

They weren't yet making the big money they would when they signed their next Sahara contract, but even so, when the time came to buy their own place, they could afford it. Though the Las Vegas Strip was booming, land in and around the city was still pretty cheap. In 1955, a 50-by-135-foot lot cost $695. Another deal offered a 100-by-300-foot lot for fifteen dollars down and fifteen dollars a month. On the high end was a three-bedroom, two-bath house with a landscaped yard for $18,250—negotiable.

What made "The Wildest" work onstage was that every member of the band contributed, knowing his or her role. But all followed Louis's lead. He became the performer he was apparently born to be, and he reveled in being the center of the musical storm.

According to Segreto, Prima "had an extraordinary ability to feel the pulse of the audience, and not only to feel the pulse of the audience but to almost create a pulse for the audience."

"The most important thing was that the music never stopped even in between songs," said Will Friedwald in *Louis Prima: The Wildest!*. "Even during announcements and things like that, the tempo always kept going. Everything was always to the beat. And it just kept everything at this really high energy level."

"The Chief always opened his show with 'When You're Smiling' and he always closed the show with 'When the Saints Go Marching In,' but always what happened in between there, each and every show, was completely different," said Segreto.

Sam Butera said, "When we walked on stage, we didn't know what we were going to do. He called out the songs and we hit 'em."

"I may have seen his show thousands of times," said Segreto, "and no one show was the same."

"He always managed to keep it on a very high dynamic," Friedwald said. "He always kept the excitement level going no matter what. So you were always sitting at the edge of your seat at a Prima show."

Fifty years later, George Guida, in a lengthy essay in the *Journal of Popular Culture*, tried from an academic perspective to describe what the Louis-Keely dynamic was and why it worked:

Keely Smith is an American Madonna, part Irish, part English, part American Indian (the part she has always put to stage use); in her day, Smith personified stoic sexuality. Raven-haired, somewhere between tawny and fair, "at once nut brown and pixieish," she was a hybrid goddess: both 1950s American ice queen and classical object of male devotion, ideal of feminine reserve and idol of seductive motherhood.

Louis Prima was an Italian boy. And Italian boys, probably all boys, at some point approach their mothers with a combination of fear, respect, worship and sexual desire. This was Prima's approach to Smith on the Las Vegas stage. While his goddess stood stock still, the "ethnic bad boy" leapt around, shuffled, pumped his fists in the air, danced to the wild music of his band, and occasionally blew his horn with all the enthusiasm, if not the technique, of his namesake and "hero," Louis Armstrong. Prima played the rambunctious child for his mother/lover Smith's approval, which came in the form of laughter, mock Italian gestures, and calls of "Oh, Luigi"—but came only rarely, and then only briefly. Smith herself stood, literally, for American beauty, America—both white and Native—to be made, New World consummation devoutly to be wished, obtainable but always at a certain distance from the Italian (ethnic) American who, like Prima, still spoke the language of his people.

Bottom line: They kicked butt onstage, and the audiences laughed with them and loved them.

In more layman's terms, the comedian Shecky Greene remembers, "Louis had animal magnetism. He was not a beautiful man, but the women would go crazy for him. He was just a great showman, and everything he did appeared perfect for grabbing an audience. And Keely—she would just stand there and what was so smart is that was the only way you would put your eyes on Keely, and once you did, it was hard to take your eyes off her and bring them back to Louis or maybe Sam blowing the sax. Years later, when I saw Sonny and Cher, it was like seeing Louis and Keely all over again."

An important extra ingredient is that everyone believed that Louis and Keely were very much in love, and they did nothing to dispel that. They were together almost all the time, on- and offstage (an exception being when Louis played golf). They didn't discuss their romance with the press because, when not performing, Louis was all business and Keely simply was not likely to talk about her personal life.

"Offstage, I was very shy, I didn't talk to anybody," Keely reflected years later about her early days in Las Vegas. "During intermission, I would go to the ladies room to read a book. Even when Sinatra was in the audience, I'd say hello and then disappear into the restroom."

The record companies were convinced that "The Wildest" was not a flash in the pan. It was a new and original act that was doing turn-away business and represented the new brand of Las Vegas entertainment that moved beyond the late-career acts of Sophie Tucker, Rudy Vallee, Ray Bolger, and

Jimmy Durante (also from New Orleans), though these performers remained popular on the Strip and had regular return engagements.

"The Wildest" was so popular that the Sahara didn't have to worry that it drew people away from the gaming tables into the Casbar Lounge; the act was attracting a lot of people who might otherwise have gone to another hotel. With five shows a night patrons might have to wait until the third or even fifth show to get in, so they might as well play blackjack or roulette or the slots while they waited. Or they could catch the earlier entertainment in the hotel. For $6.75, a patron could both enjoy a New York steak dinner and see Abbott & Costello's show in the Congo Room, the hotel's main show-room. For a casino, a possible concern was that the lounge act was becoming more popular than the main acts in the Congo Room, but as long as the main room kept filling up, that was simply an embarrassment of riches for owner Milton Prell and his backers.

Prima signed on with Capitol Records, which had Frank Sinatra, who was in the process of changing American music, as its biggest star. Sinatra may have helped to bring his fellow *paisan* and Las Vegas showman into the fold simply because he thought Prima's surging popularity would sell records. But he also saw in him a guy who had been down on his luck and practically had to beg to keep his career going. Prima had called Bill Miller and was willing to take anything. Sinatra had signed a recording contract that paid only a thousand dollars, and he had to pay his own expenses. Then he won the Academy Award for playing the doomed Angelo Maggio in the number-one film of 1953.

Being with Capitol after the success of *From Here to Eternity* gave Sinatra "his greatest role: his own musical and stylistic reinvention," wrote Benjamin Schwartz in "His Second Act," an essay published in 2007 in the *Atlantic*. "The 16 concept albums that followed, his most remarkable achievement and among America's enduring cultural treasures, defied public taste and redirected it toward what would be known as the Great American Songbook. With his key collaborator, Nelson Riddle, Sinatra jettisoned the yearning, sweet-voiced crooning of his Columbia years in favor of a richer voice, greater rhythmic invention, and more knowing and conversational phrasing."

Keely was being a trouper, apparently willing and able to be onstage right up until she went into labor. It helped that she was the youngest person on the stage, and she sure didn't slow the rest of the band down. *Fabulous Las Vegas* in its February 19 edition referred to Louis and Keely "who, with their 'witnesses,' manage to set the whole room into a turmoil each and every night."

"Meet me in the Casbar" was the line of copy above "Louis Prima with Keely Smith and Kay Martin Trio" in a print ad. What was unusual and a sign of the act's rapid ascent was that the advertisement was for an appearance by Mae West in the Sahara's Congo Room. The lounge was no longer an afterthought but another attraction drawing people to the hotel.

Because of the advanced pregnancy, Louis and Keely had to shut the show down toward the end of February. It had to be a bittersweet moment for Louis especially. He had taken big steps on the comeback trail, he was playing pretty for the people once again, his third child was soon to be born, he had a beautiful and talented wife, he had a foot-stomping band behind him . . . and he had to go sit on the sidelines.

Louis left the small stage with a generous gesture. "What a closing performance!" exclaimed Jack Cortez in *Fabulous Las Vegas*. "We're speaking of Louis Prima's final night of his Casbar engagement at the Hotel Sahara. The last show went on until six ayem. Prima bought drinks for everyone in attendance and the figure was close to two hundred and fifty (250). Everyone stood up and drank a farewell toast to Louis, his wife Keely and the child which will soon join the Prima clan."

Two weeks later Keely, showing the same impeccable timing she had onstage, gave birth to Antoinette Elizabeth Prima on March 9, her own twenty-seventh birthday.

18

"The Wildest" wasn't supposed to return until May 17, 1955, but the act was in such demand that Keely rushed back to the stage before the end of April. "This past week, Keely Smith and Louis Prima returned to the Casbar, for an unlimited engagement," *Fabulous Las Vegas* reported. "Charles Boyer may have convinced a few women of the merits of the Casbar, but Louis and his wife have convinced an untold number that the Hotel Sahara lounge is the place to visit. A great ovation greeted them when they opened. It was fantastic to watch their many fans and friends attempt to crowd into spaces that were already taken."

They quickly settled back into a groove, thanks in large part to their rigorous schedule. In addition to whatever rehearsal Louis demanded and the instructions he gave them, the band learned by doing.

Keely reiterated in *Cult Vegas*, "Everything we did, we found onstage— including all the lines that Sam used to throw. The deadpan look was because we did five 45-minute shows, and I was up there about a half-hour each show before I even opened my mouth. I didn't know what to do with myself. So I used to just fold my arms, cross my legs, and lean up against the piano. And I watched everything that went on in the room, and the casino too. And then when Louis would come and pull on my skirt, he would be disrupting what I was watching, and I'd look down at him like, 'Don't bother me.'"

Sam would usually get his turn in the show before Keely, after Louis brayed and danced his way through several songs that had long been in his repertoire.

"In general the next thing would be Sam Butera," recalled Joe Segreto. "Sam had a segment in the show where Louis would introduce Sam, and Sam would do one or two of his numbers that could be a vocal or an instrumental."

Writer Nick Tosches—whose biography of Jerry Lee Lewis, *Balls of Fire*, is a classic—observed in *Louis Prima: The Wildest!* that "Sam's version of 'Night Train' is like the killer version." He added, "Musically, in the relationship between Louie and Keely, Keely was the sweetener. Keely would sweetly come in and sing a little bit in English softly and nicely, a total contrast to Louis."

"The lovely Keely would provide her husband with both a stoic, stone-faced counterpoint to his comic antics and a duet partner capable of matching him stride for stride," wrote Joseph F. Laredo. "There came a moment in each show, however, when she would take center stage to perform a popular standard with such skill and soulful conviction that the audience grew quiet and hushed, and everyone sitting in the dark and smoky room was made fully aware that the sensitive stylist in the spotlight was a ballad singer of the very highest order."

But Keely could be raucous too. According to a press item, "A real 'ball' was had by all who attended the Casbar at the Hotel Sahara, last Saturday ayem. Deadpan songstress-comedienne Keely Smith (Mrs. Louis Prima) let loose with all her hilarious nature and broke up everyone in the place, including the musicians."

Still, Louis was the Chief at all times. Improvisation was fine within the parameters he set.

"He was a master at lining the show up," Keely said about him. "He would feature himself in the first three songs, then he'd feature the trombone player, then the bass player or sometimes the drummer. Then Sam, then me, then he and I would close the show together."

Those who marveled at Prima's stamina were not privy to how he "prepared" for each show. "He would fall asleep, just like that," said Butera. "Showtime, he would wake up and go on stage. I can't do that. There's certain people who can, you know, just fall asleep for a few minutes, and that's what he did."

"When that curtain would go up, if that audience wasn't paying very close attention, he'd make the curtain come back down," said Segreto.

According to Lou Sino, who spent ten years as Prima's trombone player beginning in 1957, "I've seen him nights, when that curtain went up and he didn't get that response he wanted, he said, 'Bring the curtain back down again,' and if the curtain went up again and the audience was still dead, 'Bring that curtain down again.'"

"The audience would finally get hip to what he was doing," Segreto said, "and then he would swing it and knock the back of the house up."

"I even saw him stop in the middle of a song and switch to another song because he knew instinctively it wasn't going to work and he'd take another path," says Hunt-Bono.

Las Vegas was already known as a late-night town, but "The Wildest" brought that to a new level. "The horn blows at midnight in the Casbar Lounge" headlined an advertisement for the show in 1956. With short breaks in between they would perform until 6:00 A.M., which for some of the year was dawn or after.

"Prima did more than anyone except Sinatra to fuel Vegas' image as a wild all-night party," wrote Mike Weatherford in *Cult Vegas*. "Prima didn't invent the lounge any more than Sinatra invented the showroom; he was just in the right place at the right time. But it was Prima who became the quintessential lounge act and put the Sahara's Casbar on the cocktail napkin of history as 'The Wildest Show in Vegas.'"

Some of the items that appeared in the Las Vegas press with increasing frequency about the act were planted by Prima himself. He found new outlets for the promotional energy he had displayed as a big-band leader. As one rival commented, "Louis was the only guy I know of who ever played Vegas that was able to get a quote from Howard Hughes for running in an ad on a billboard, and the quote was, 'Every time I see them, they get better.'"

Prima was also increasingly asserting himself, even within the Sahara itself, as he became more of a Las Vegas insider and "The Wildest" brought in more revenue.

"The pit bosses were coming to Louis and telling him, 'You have to be quiet, you have to turn the sound down,'" Butera recalled in *Cult Vegas*. "Louis would get very perturbed because what we were trying to get across was energy—make these people happy and make them want to stay there and enjoy themselves. It got to such a point that Louis said one night, 'Pack up your things, we're going home.' That's the way Louis Prima was—he wouldn't take seconds from nobody, not if he thought he was right. He had to prove a point. Sure enough, we didn't work the next night. Then they came to Louis and said, 'There's no people in the lounge.' They came and begged him to come back to work."

They must have enjoyed the night off. Somehow, Louis and Keely and Sam and the band kept to the brutal schedule of midnight to six, six days a week. Typically, lounge engagements were not that long, but, with "The Wildest," the Sahara couldn't afford to give them a break. According to one print account toward the end of July, "It seems as though every night it's New Year's Eve at the Sahara's Casbar Lounge. Louis Prima and Keely Smith are playing to standing-room only (ten deep)."

People from out of town put seeing the act high on their lists. The word of mouth that tourists took back home to Minnesota and Pennsylvania and Texas was excellent. Because of the small space and the personalities onstage, the audience could feel part of the act.

"We have a lot of lounge acts that are very cold and very indifferent to the audience," Keely told National Public Radio in a September 2007 interview to coincide with the release of the CD *Keely Smith: The Essential Capitol Collection*. "We talked to our audience. The audience was allowed to ask us questions. They were allowed to interact with us onstage. Nobody ever called me Ms. Smith, it was always Keely. Nobody ever called Louis Mr. Prima. That's what our lounge act was, it was one big living room."

Certainly Prima's success in Las Vegas encouraged casino operators to put out the welcome mat to New Orleans musicians. At least once, his brother played the Casbar Lounge when "The Wildest" took a break, but, unlike Louis, Leon didn't embrace the Las Vegas lifestyle. He preferred to stay put in the Big Easy. In November 1955, Jack Teagarden had made his Strip debut in the Stagebar at the Flamingo Hotel. Soon a new generation led by Al Hirt and Pete Fountain would be making appearances. Perhaps as much as New Orleans itself, Las Vegas exposed more people to the blend of Dixieland and other forms of jazz from the South.

The *Las Vegas Review-Journal* published a photo in its December 23, 1955, issue of Louis being presented with a huge birthday cake by Milton Prell. Only a little more than a year before, Prell might have wondered about Bill Miller's sanity when he offered a seemingly washed-up Prima a two-week gig in the lounge. Now Louis, with his arm around Keely, was being honored by the top man at the Hotel Sahara. (Prell would do the honors for Keely and Antoinette, called Toni, too the following March.)

The caption underneath reads: "These all-time attendance record holders for Las Vegas lounges are back by popular demand in the Sahara's Casbar Lounge. Louis' versatility, complemented by the fresh song styling of Keely, make this combo one of the newest innovations in show business today."

What a difference a year made. A few weeks later, as 1956 began, Prell would order that the Casbar Lounge be completely remodeled, adding a revolving stage and increasing seating capacity. Fittingly, "The Wildest" was going to get even wilder and bigger that year.

19

———

Up and down the Strip the neon glowed, illuminating the signs that shouted the names of the casinos featuring headliners who found awestruck audiences in the desert. Some performers, like Louis and Keely, were reaching for or were at their peak—Liberace at the Riviera Hotel, Carmen Miranda at the New Frontier (one of her skirts contained eighty-five thousand sequins), Frankie Laine at the Desert Inn, Martin and Lewis at the Sands—while others, such as the Ritz Brothers at the Flamingo Hotel, Jerry Lester at the Dunes, and Louis Jordan at the Sands, had found a second career in Las Vegas (with Prima falling into that category too).

But of all the acts drawing crowds in the mid-1950s, there was no one more important in Las Vegas than Frank Sinatra. It could be argued that Meyer Lansky or Sam Giancana or any one of the other top mobsters were more important because they controlled most of the money. But people didn't travel hundreds or thousands of miles to see mob kingpins lounging by the pool, puffing on fat cigars. They came to see Sinatra, either onstage or at the tables in the casino. And he was to have a powerful impact on the careers of Louis Prima and Keely Smith.

"Sinatra was a pop music legend, not a civic leader or entrepreneur, [but he] was a one-man chamber of commerce who gave Las Vegas something equally important: an image," wrote Mike Weatherford in the *Las Vegas*

Review-Journal. "And he did so in the mid-1950s, before demographics and visitor volume were buzzwords. It was a simpler day in a smaller town, and Sinatra's magic was more easily described: gambling, womanizing, drinking till dawn—and all of it with style."

Sinatra became close to Keely, and she idolized him. Years later there would be more than friendship—the two talked of marriage—but during the 1950s there were only rumors, which Keely contended were untrue. Sinatra was tight with Louis too. He could relate to his fellow Italian American entertainer who had tasted the heights of fame, fallen far, and had come back.

When Las Vegas was first starting to take off in the early 1950s, Sinatra was at the lowest point in his life. Such recent films as *Meet Danny Wilson* and *Miracle of the Bells* had bombed. His records had stopped selling, and he was reduced to recording novelty songs for Mitch Miller at the Columbia label—including one in which he did a duet with a barking dog—that were as popular as a week-old cannoli. (Before heading to Vegas, Prima had also recorded for Miller, then stormed out of the studio, vowing never to work with him again.) Sinatra was already a has-been at concert halls; the Chez Paree in Chicago fit 1,200 people, but when Sinatra sang there only 150 showed up. He was working on a broken heart because Ava Gardner kept threatening to leave him. (She eventually did, after seeing a newspaper photograph of him with two showgirls at a party in Las Vegas.)

But Harry Cohn at Columbia Pictures was persuaded to OK casting Sinatra instead of Eli Wallach in *From Here to Eternity.* Gardner had used her influence, and Frank had begged Jack Entratter, the front man for mobsters Frank Costello and Joey Adonis at the Sands (the latter was Cohn's fishing buddy), to pitch him for the picture. When the movie was a huge hit and Frank's portrayal of Maggio won him the Academy Award for Best Supporting Actor, his star rose once again. Fast.

He signed a deal with Capitol Records in 1953 that would last until 1961, and many consider this period his finest as a recording star, working with Nelson Riddle as his arranger. His first album for the label, *Songs for Young Lovers*, released in '54, was a hit along with the first single released from it, "Young at Heart," which was also the title of a popular movie he made with Doris Day. That year, in the year-end poll conducted by *Downbeat* magazine, he was voted the most popular male vocalist of the year, earning the title for the first time since 1947.

With his financial fortunes happily reversed, Sinatra paid fifty-four thousand dollars for a 2 percent stake in the Sands. Over time, his investment would expand to 9 percent, and that alone made him a multimillionaire. Among the other owners with Costello and Adonis were Lansky, Gerardo Catena, acting boss of the Genovese family in New York, and Joe Fusco, a former protégé of Al Capone.

Las Vegas was a playground for Sinatra as well as a source of revenue. He was royalty in the city, and he was both revered and feared along the Strip. In addition to the house he owned in Palm Springs, he liked to entertain his friends at his new home away from home.

"Frank used to call me up and ask me if I wanted to go to Vegas with him that weekend," recalled Tony Curtis in his memoir *American Prince*. "He'd come by my house in his Karmann Ghia, and off we'd go. It was Frank who put the Sands Hotel on the map. When Frank started showing up at the Sands to perform, the Sands became *the* place to be seen. He sang there without a contract. When he was finished with his gig there, Frank would return home carrying a duffel bag full of cash. I don't know how they did it—there were no mobile phones in those days—but whenever Frank and I drove up to the Sands, a greeting party was always standing outside waiting."

"I used to stop always at the Sands, just to hang out," recalls Debbie Reynolds. "And as a lark, sometimes get up and sing and do impressions with Frank and Sammy and whoever else was around."

Though he still had to endure the vestiges of racism and segregation laws, another major Las Vegas headliner was Sammy Davis Jr. He had first performed there in 1945 as part of the Will Mastin Trio with his father and uncle. Out of loyalty, it remained the Will Mastin Trio for another ten years, though it was evident to everyone that Davis, with his singing and dancing and imitations, was by far the star of the group.

If you made it in New York or Los Angeles or both in the mid-1950s, the next stop was Las Vegas. "In early 1957 I was the headliner at the opening of the new Tropicana Hotel in Las Vegas," recounted Eddie Fisher in his autobiography, *Been There, Done That*. "In less than a decade Las Vegas had grown from a small oasis in the desert into a mecca of neon lights, gambling, and beautiful girls. It had become *the* destination for high rollers from everywhere in the world, an American Monte Carlo. Organized crime built it, with the help of entertainers like Sinatra, and owned it. . . . Mike Todd had once warned me against playing Vegas, but that was one of the few times I didn't listen to him."

Appearing regularly at the height of their fame as movie stars and as a nightclub act were Martin and Lewis. Audiences on the Strip couldn't get enough of the combination of Dean Martin, the smooth straight man and crooner, and Jerry Lewis, who was a loud and totally unpredictable physical comic. For as long as they stayed together, they commanded top dollar.

Their start in Vegas had not been an auspicious one, at least not for Lewis. In September 1949, they were booked into the Flamingo Hotel for a week at fifteen thousand dollars. The recently married Martin brought his wife, but Lewis's remained in Los Angeles. Left on his own when not performing, the twenty-three-year-old Lewis greeted the gambling opportunities with gusto. By the end of the week he was over a hundred thousand dollars in debt.

When confronted by the crew that had taken over the hotel from Bugsy Siegel, Lewis wisely vowed to repay it. He claims that he did, in less than three years, every penny. And he never gambled there again.

As one hotel and casino after another opened on and near the Strip, the demand for entertainers grew rapidly. If you had some talent and name recognition, you could get a job. It might not be in the main showroom, but you were getting paid to entertain people who in larger numbers were coming from all over the country.

Las Vegas was a place where one could find the composer and conductor Andre Previn moonlighting as a jazzman. Michael Freedland reported in his biography of Previn, "One Christmas, Andre and his trio were playing in the lounge of a Las Vegas hotel. It wasn't most people's idea of festive surroundings for the festive season. No number of girls in short costumes dressed as Santa Claus in the middle of a heat wave can really compensate for the traditional Yuletide. Yet here he was surrounded by walls without windows, decorations without clocks and everywhere the slot machines."

Ray Bolger, who played the Scarecrow in 1939's *The Wizard of Oz*, found new life in Las Vegas as a song-and-dance man. One of more recent vintage,

Donald O'Connor, headlined in the Sahara's Congo Room. Judy Garland herself made her Las Vegas debut in July 1956 at the New Frontier Hotel. Orson Welles made his first nightclub appearance at the Riviera Hotel in February 1957. Shortly before, Betty Grable and Harry James had formed an act for an engagement at the Hotel El Rancho Vegas, and had warmed up by seeing Louis and Keely perform at the Sahara and joining them on the crowded stage. One of Louis's old flames was in town when, according to one account, "Martha Raye arrived to visit her 'dream man,' Al Riddle, dealer at the Hotel Sahara."

As Sammy Davis Jr. found, Las Vegas was a good place to build a career and emerge as a star as long as he could stand insults like not being allowed to stay at the same hotel where he performed. By the 1950s, Davis had seen and experienced plenty of bigotry. The son of a black dancer and a Puerto Rican chorus girl, in 1943 he served in the U.S. Army's first integrated unit. His nose was broken repeatedly in fistfights with bigger white soldiers. He was able to transfer to an entertainment unit, and after the war he formed a trio with his father and a man he considered his uncle, and the Will Mastin trio wound up in Las Vegas.

"When the trio arrived in Las Vegas, they were treated like anyone else on stage," wrote Matt Birkbeck in *Deconstructing Sammy*. "But when the music ended and the crowd disappeared, they were black again and forced to sleep in hotels on the segregated west side of town. Sammy sat in his room late at night, looking out at the lights on the Strip, knowing he was barred from entering any of the hotels or casinos there."

"By the late 1930s, despite their growing importance to the community's infant resort industry, blacks faced more segregationist barriers," wrote Eugene P. Moehring. "Although southern dam workers were gone, tourists (many of them southerners transplanted to California) increasingly expected southern Nevada to mirror the Jim Crow atmosphere of not only Dixie but the rest of the nation. In response, Fremont Street clubs increasingly barred 'negroes' from the bars and gaming tables." An integration of public accommodations bill died in committee in the Nevada state assembly. "In the meantime, blacks now found themselves being denied service not only in hotels, but also in a growing number of restaurants and stores."

Lena Horne recalled in her autobiography written with Richard Schickel being the subject of prejudice not so much from casino owners and audiences as fellow musicians.

When she was booked at the Flamingo soon after it opened, "I made what amounted to a pioneering trek to Las Vegas—pioneering in the sense that I was the first Negro to star in a big club there and pioneering, also, in the sense that I went there right at the beginning of the expansion and glamorization of the big clubs on the strip."

Horne shared the bill with a well-known Latin band, the leader of which was deliberately rude to her. When she threatened to walk out on the engagement, her fiancé, Lennie Hayton, placed a call to the Flamingo's manager, who was less than enthusiastic about stirring up trouble. Then Hayton heard another voice on the line: "I didn't know she was having any trouble," Bugsy Siegel said. "She will not have any further trouble."

During subsequent shows, the bandleader couldn't have been more polite. However, another account has it that while Siegel allowed Horne to stay in a cabana near the Flamingo, he had the maids burn her bed linens every morning.

Not only could black and white patrons still not share tables in the lounges, black customers could not place bets in the casinos. Sammy Davis Jr. had to stand behind a white friend placing bets for him. When in 1955 Dorothy Dandridge played the Hotel Last Frontier, Pearl Bailey was at the Flamingo, Billy Eckstine sang at the Sands, and Lionel Hampton and his troupe performed at the Moulin Rouge, none could stay in any of the rooms upstairs. So it was a coup for Horne that after making her debut at the Sands soon after it opened, she was able to live in one of the rooms for the duration of her engagement. Another time while at the Sands, Marlene Dietrich grabbed Horne's arm and pulled her into the casino bar for a drink, and no one challenged the two stars.

Las Vegas was often referred to in the early to mid-'50s as the "Mississippi of the West" by black performers, and there seemed no end to the indignities—Davis had to stay with a black family across town, and Nat King Cole could not have dinner in the hotel where he headlined (while his supporting act at the Sands, the comedians Dan Rowan and Dick Martin, could). But they wanted to be hired there because of the money. Before Horne had

had enough of Vegas, she was earning twenty-five thousand dollars a week. Certainly there was more money and more opportunity for talented black entertainers in Las Vegas than there was on Broadway.

Taking a big financial step forward in July 1956 was Nat King Cole. Jack Entratter at the Sands signed him to a contract that called for a series of engagements into 1959 for five hundred thousand dollars. In the year-end issue of *Fabulous Las Vegas*, the publication made this Christmas wish: "To Nat King Cole and Louis Prima, an extra large over-size money belt (my, those contracts!)."

A pioneer in Las Vegas desegregation was Allard Roen, who in the 1950s was the managing director of the Desert Inn. When the black U.S. diplomat and Nobel Peace Prize recipient Ralph Bunche wanted to visit Vegas, Roen reserved a room for him at the Desert Inn and escorted him to it. He extended golf privileges to Sammy Davis Jr. for use of the resort's course. He also met Pearl Bailey's request that she be able to use an all-black chorus line. In 1960, he negotiated an agreement with the NAACP to open the Desert Inn and Stardust officially to minority guests.

As Prima found out, Vegas was a place where careers could be remade. In 1956, in the wake of his acrimonious split with Dean Martin, Jerry Lewis went to Vegas to recuperate with his wife and another couple. They stayed at the Sands for four days. He and his former partner as well as their handlers worried if either of the men had a career left with the act finished.

As Lewis was packing to leave he received a call from Sid Luft telling him that Luft's wife, Judy Garland, was too ill to go onstage at the Frontier Hotel. Any chance Lewis could fill in, like, now?

Perhaps the suddenness allowed Lewis not to think about being a solo act and, of course, not having a solo act to do. He said he would be right over. He threw on a blue suit and borrowed a pair of black socks. When he got backstage and after being greeted by a sobbing Garland, the orchestra struck up "Over the Rainbow," and there was even a "Miss Judy Garland" introduction. But out walked Jerry Lewis, blinking into the lights. "I don't look much like Judy, do I?" he asked.

The audience agreed and found that very funny. Lewis improvised for an hour, which included singing songs that had once been Martin's exclusive territory. He closed by doing an imitation of Jolson singing "Rock-a-bye

Your Baby with a Dixie Melody." When he walked off to cheers, Lewis had begun a career as one of the most successful performers on the Strip for years to come. That December he did three weeks at the Sands. This was an unhappy occurrence to part-owner Sinatra, who supported his friend Dino, but Lewis earned every cent of the twenty-five thousand a week he received. (The following year Garland, in the midst of one of her many comebacks, had her eleven-year-old daughter join her for a duet onstage at the Flamingo, and thus Liza Minnelli made her Las Vegas debut.)

Also not necessarily predictable but better planned was Martin's new career phase as a solo performer at the Sands. He had just made a movie, *Ten Thousand Bedrooms*, with Gina Lollobrigida, that failed financially and critically. Some observers in showbiz contended that Dean had been little more than a Bud Abbott–like straight man for the more talented Jerry. Martin had a nice-enough voice, and maybe he would have a modest career at best on his own. In darker moments, Martin believed that too. But he also realized that if he did no more than sing he would be perceived as only half an act, and he had to do something about that.

He hired Ed Simmons, a comedy writer who had just also dissolved a partnership, with Norman Lear (who would go on to TV fame with *All in the Family*, *The Jeffersons*, and other hit shows). He and Martin created a soused saloon singer character, and wrote jokes accordingly. Then it was time to hit the stage.

"Dean's opening night at the Sands was something," recalled Shirley MacLaine in *My Lucky Stars*. "It was well attended by celebrities because we wanted to be there for him. We were nervous because there but for the grace of God could go any of us. What would he do as a single? Many already thought he was a has-been."

Instead, Martin was a comeback kid. He walked out onstage with a glass of scotch in one hand and a cigarette in the other and told the audience, "Drink up—the drunker you get, the better I sound." His act alternated between offhand jokes and songs, many with lyrics altered for comic effect. "The audience adored him," reported MacLaine, "particularly those of us in show business. We understood what a breakthrough he had made. He had found who he was comfortable being."

Louis Prima (center) was only sixteen years old when he formed this band in New Orleans in 1927 that featured (left to right) Irving Fazola, John Miller, Bob Jeffers, George Hartman, Cliff LeBlanc, Leonart Albersted, Jacob Sciambra, Burt Andrus, and John Viviano.
LOUISIANA STATE MUSEUM JAZZ COLLECTION

Prima hit the big time in New York at the Famous Door nightclub in New York City in 1935 with the New Orleans Gang, which featured a brilliant sideman, Pee Wee Russell (top right), on clarinet.
BETTMANN/CORBIS

Prima's trumpet playing complemented the singing of Alice Faye in the 1939 musical *Rose of Washington Square*.

One of the more
alluring portraits
of Louis Prima,
taken in 1940, when
he continued to be
especially popular
among women.

A portrait of Keely Smith taken
early in her career as Louis Prima's
featured singer.

(left and below) While the Mary Kaye Trio and other acts had made hotel lounges in Las Vegas more appealing, when "The Wildest" first hit the Casbar Lounge in the Sahara Hotel in 1954, the act was original and immediately popular.

Louis and Keely celebrate Louis's birthday at the Sahara Hotel. It didn't take them long to become the most popular husband-and-wife act in Las Vegas.

A portrait of Louis and Keely that certainly does not indicate that there was an almost eighteen-year age difference between them.
GETTY IMAGES

Part of the appeal of the Prima-Smith-Butera band was its humor, which spilled over to the design of their album covers. There were times when Prima's voice was compared to that of a moose.

When "The Wildest" went on the road, the act was just as popular as it was in Las Vegas. Here, with Sam Butera on sax, in his usual spot to Prima's left, they play a concert in Los Angeles in January 1958.
GETTY IMAGES

A still from the 1958 film *Thunder Road*, in which Keely played Robert Mitchum's love interest.

Louis was known as tight with a dollar, but from time to time he splurged on Keely, such as with a mink coat.

A tender moment between the two leads in the 1959 movie *Hey Boy! Hey Girl!*

Four of the main members of the Rat Pack on stage at the Sands Hotel: Dean Martin, Frank Sinatra, Sammy Davis Jr., and Joey Bishop.
UNLV LIBRARIES, SPECIAL COLLECTIONS

Dean Martin entertains a packed house full of celebrities, including Jack Benny (standing) and Debbie Reynolds and Shirley MacLaine (seated right). UNLV LIBRARIES, SPECIAL COLLECTIONS

This pleasing portrait of Louis and Keely was taken in 1961. Ironically, it was the image sent to many news outlets to accompany articles about their divorce later that year.
BETTMANN/CORBIS

Louis and the singer who would become his fifth wife, Gia Maione, and the band performed on Ed Sullivan's Sunday evening show in 1962. BETTMANN/CORBIS

Twist All Night, released in 1961, had Louis gyrating with much younger women in an effort to capture a new audience after his split from Keely.

Keely's comeback record was her tribute to Frank Sinatra, whom she has called one of the loves of her life. The album earned her a Grammy Award nomination for Best Female Vocal at age seventy-one.

Keely is congratulated by singers Karen Akers (left) and Phoebe Snow after the opening night of a four-week engagement at the Carlyle Hotel in New York in April 2007. PHOTO BY MARK RUPP

But number one on anybody's list of acts to see was Sinatra, and to do that you had to go to the Sands. "Soon, the Sands was *the* place," recalled Nancy Sinatra in her memoir *Frank Sinatra: My Father.*

Jack Entratter, Nick Kelly, Carl Cohen, they were quite a team. They knew what talent to book, what food to serve. They also knew how to be generous, and they weren't afraid to be. There were always free drinks for the gamblers. . . . On special occasions there were bags of silver dollars for guests. There was the Chuck Wagon—all you can eat for a dollar. There was an easygoing feeling that doesn't exist anymore. Of course, thirty-dollar plane rides don't exist anymore either. Or fifteen-dollar rooms.

Dean, Sammy, Danny Thomas, Jerry Lewis, Red Skelton—the whole roster was exciting. The casual mood prevailed. From building to building. No ties, no codes. Each building was named for a racetrack: Churchill Downs, Hollywood Park, Hialeah. Dad had an apartment there that would be our Las Vegas home for many years. . . . Dad was the hottest attraction in a hot town.

Sinatra was entering his peak years as an entertainer, and he found his greatest success in Hollywood and Las Vegas. On the big screen in the mid-1950s he was seen in *Young at Heart* with Doris Day, *Guys and Dolls* with Marlon Brando and Jean Simmons, *The Man with the Golden Arm* (which earned him his second Oscar nomination, this time in the Best Actor category), *High Society* with Bing Crosby and Grace Kelly, and *The Joker Is Wild*, about longtime Vegas comedian Joe E. Lewis, who performed often at the Sands, sometimes reciting Shakespeare with Sinatra.

And there was Elvis too. He would become a regular in Las Vegas late in his career, but his debut there was not promising at all. He was twenty-one in April 1956 and had just completed his first sessions for RCA Records. "Heartbreak Hotel" was getting radio play, and he had made his first television appearance, on the *Dorsey Brothers TV Show.* Presley was booked to appear at the New Frontier Hotel on a bill with Shecky Greene and Freddy Martin and his orchestra. To help hype the relatively unknown man from Memphis, he was proclaimed in print ads to be "The Atomic Powered Singer." (Greene became friends with both Louis and Keely, and for a time employed Louis's daughter Joyce. "He was not happy about that," Greene says. "I don't think he wanted her in show business.")

People didn't come to Las Vegas to see rock 'n' roll then, as evidenced by the tepid reception Presley received. He did two twelve-minute shows a night for two weeks. Even dressing him up in a bow tie and jacket didn't help him blend in. Elsewhere in 1956 his career took off, especially when he appeared on Milton Berle's TV show and Ed Sullivan's show, which was seen by fifty-four million viewers. When he returned to Las Vegas later that year, it was to see Liberace's show at the Riviera and Freddie Bell and his Bellboys at the Sands. Presley was particularly captivated by Bell because of a song he sang that began, "You ain't nothin' but a hound dog!" It had been recorded in 1953 by Big Mama Thornton and was written by two white teenagers, Mike Stoller and Jerry Leiber.

Apparently, there was another popular act in Las Vegas that Elvis enjoyed. After Presley's "All Shook Up" climbed to the top of the charts, he was asked where he got the wiggle that went with performing it. "From Louis Prima, of course," he replied.

20

In the time before Steve Lawrence and Eydie Gormé, it was rare for a Las Vegas headlining act to consist of a husband and wife. You could find them on television, with notable examples being George Burns and Gracie Allen and Lucille Ball and Desi Arnaz, and such fictional pairings as Ralph Kramden and his wife, Alice, on *The Honeymooners*. But Las Vegas was about single performers, or those who wanted to convey a single reputation.

That was a big reason why Louis and Keely were different. They were married. They appeared to have fun together. With Antoinette they were a family. They were in love and had passion for each other that no one thought was feigned.

"He was extremely sexy," Keely said about her husband. "He had something about him that was almost animalistic. He was so intense and had such command of the music and his audience. And the way he moved his legs—you know, he was the original Elvis Presley."

Women in the audience might still be swooning, but Keely would not swoon onstage. That she appeared impervious to his charms upped the sexual tension in the act. How could she not give in? And when the time finally came when she did, the earth must have moved.

"Perhaps no other husband-and-wife team had been as successful in American popular music," wrote Garry Boulard. "Productive, exhaustive, and nationally visible, the Prima-Smith marriage seemed like a Hollywood treatment of romance and happy endings. One of the imponderables of their success undoubtedly was the role their very public private lives played in their careers. Fans and friends wondered what it was like in the Prima-Smith household, were they really the good friends that they seemed onstage? Were there any tensions performing together, doing business together, and living together as husband and wife? Fan magazines speculated, but the adoring masses would have none of it."

The couple wasn't talking. Keely remained shy and content in her husband's shadow. Louis, ever the businessman, knew that, like in a relationship, keeping the mystery alive meant success. And in this town, success was measured in money.

Money was what made Las Vegas tick. It flowed in and it flowed out, in some cases to hidden and overseas bank accounts. If you had it and spent it, you could get away with almost anything—even just being yourself, as a future billionaire found out.

"Once again, we spotted Howard Hughes on the local scene, garbed in his far from meticulous apparel," went a report in *Fabulous Las Vegas.* "He had a lovely, well-groomed chorine in tow. The millionaire sportsman indulged in back-line gaming at the Hotel Sahara. The dice-shooter tossed a few passes, causing tycoon Hughes to lose some of his silver dollars. In a burst of temperament, he ordered the lovely lassie to leave him, claiming she was bringing him a heap of bad luck. (This is sportsmanship? 'Tain't the way we heard it!)"

By this point, with Las Vegas enjoying a golden age of wealth and entertainment, every hotel was promoting lounge acts. "The Wildest" was anything but highbrow, but the act had made casino lounges respectable.

"The big gamblers used to seat their wives in the lounge and leave them," Keely told Mike Weatherford for his *Cult Vegas.* "And they were okay; they knew they wouldn't be touched, that nobody would try to pick them up. It gave the gambler the freedom he needed to go gamble."

Louis looked after the money that the act was raking in. He had total control of the act's finances, and he was not known for being generous with salaries.

"I really liked Louis, but I couldn't swallow some of the other things that went with him, such as being really tight with a nickel," recalls Paul Ferrara, a drummer from New Orleans who spent two years with the act, in 1958 and '59. "One time Louis got a new set of drums and every night he showed them off to the audience, like 'Look what a great bandleader I am.' One night, Barbara Belle comes to me and says, 'Paul, the Chief wants to know when you're going to make your first payment on the set of drums.' The blood rushed to my head. I said, 'Barbara, you tell the Chief for me, when he wants me to make the first payment on these drums, for him to tell me. And that'll be the day I leave this fucking job.'"

There were the occasional generous gestures, at least with his wife. One of the local columnists reported in 1956, "Over at the Sahara, Keely Smith was more enthusiastic than ever. Hubby (Louis Prima) had Santa drop a couple of mink stoles on her lily white shoulders."

If "The Wildest" was so popular, why weren't all the casinos booking the same kind of acts in their lounges? Most tried, with performers who attempted to measure up to Prima and his band. Mickey Katz and his troupe were advertised as "those madcap zanies in a riot of hilarity." There was Tony Pastor and His Singin', Swingin' Pastors. The Goofers was another attempt. The lounge at the Flamingo offered Harold Stern and His Singing Violins, who managed to get a guest stint on an *I Love Lucy* episode.

But they just didn't have the same ingredients and formula. To the audiences in Las Vegas, there was only one Keely Smith, one Sam Butera, and of course many had known and were now being convinced all over again that there was only one Louis Prima.

He was back, finally, in a studio, recording songs. In a burst of creativity, on the same day Butera wrote new arrangements for "Just a Gigolo/I Ain't Got Nobody" and "Jump, Jive, an' Wail," they were recorded in April 1956. The album containing both, titled *The Wildest*, would be out in October, and Prima would have his first big radio hit in almost a decade.

The album included "Oh Marie," "Buona Sera," and "The Lip," among others. Louis's head, mouth wide open, took up most of the cover, with his name right under the title, and in the lower left corner in smaller print was "featuring Keely Smith with Sam Butera and the Witnesses." The Chief, not the Injun—as Keely was sometimes called, especially by Sinatra—got the top credit, no questions asked.

"Much of the material had been performed by Louis and Keely for years previous, but Butera re-arranged all the selections to make them really swing," wrote Scott Shea in the liner notes to a reissued version years later. "The selections on this disc abound with Prima trademarks: sudden tempo shifts into and out of Prima's patented 'shuffle beat'; tarantellas interwoven with Dixieland jazz; medleys of re-worked standards; altered lyrics befitting Prima's dialect, and numerous passages of Louis' own inimitable scat talk."

As Capitol executives had hoped, *The Wildest* was successful outside the bounds of Las Vegas. The album hopped onto the national charts and remained there for months. Many outside of Las Vegas appreciated that Louis Prima, who had first burst on the national entertainment scene two decades and two wars ago, was back and wondered, "Who's that young girl with him? She's pretty good too."

"Just a Gigolo" became Prima's signature song, and it is more associated with him than "Sing, Sing, Sing." Originally titled "Schoner Gigolo," it was composed by Leonello Casucci in Vienna in 1930. The first U.S. recordings were by Irene Bordoni and, more successfully, by Victor Lopez and his orchestra. It had last received attention in the 1946 feature film *Lover Come Back*, starring Lucille Ball (and not to be confused with the Doris Day–Rock Hudson comedy years later).

It was time for the rest of America to be exposed to "The Wildest." In the past, that would have meant Prima and his band hitting the road, traveling thousands of miles to do shows in one city after another. While Prima did take the act to clubs and concert halls in major U.S. cities, the old barnstorming approach wasn't necessary in trying to reach a larger audience in the mid-1950s, thanks to the explosion of television.

The TV executives looked eagerly to the expanding entertainment scene of Las Vegas as a reservoir of crowd-pleasing talent. If audiences full of tourists from all over the United States were happy with your act at the Sahara, Sands, or Tropicana, it stood to reason that the larger demographic of a TV audience would want to see your act too. It would be a plus if you made headlines, though not in a negative way.

Money was thrown at Frank Sinatra to do television. Dean Martin was given his own show. Milton Berle had been at the top of the TV heap for years. A successful engagement in Las Vegas meant getting a call to give TV a shot. It became Louis's turn, though it was his wife who made a special impression on the small screen.

"The major and altogether delightful surprise on Dean Martin's variety show Saturday evening on Channel 4 was the performance of Keely Smith, in private life the wife of Louis Prima, the bandleader," wrote Jack Gould in the October 7, 1957, edition of the *New York Times*. "Miss Smith, a young woman with a striking gaminelike quality, displayed not only a fine sense of comedy but also a distinctive voice of attractive huskiness. She easily stole the show."

Other popular programs on that week in the expanding television world were *The Big Record* hosted by Patti Page with Julie London and Paul Whiteman as guests, *The Rosemary Clooney Show* featuring an appearance by William Bendix, who had scored a TV hit with *The Life of Riley, Art Linkletter's House Party*, and broadcasts of the New York Yankees and the Milwaukee Braves games in the World Series (which would be won by the Braves).

The Sahara had already made sure that Louis and Keely didn't stray too far. In August 1956, Louis had signed a contract with the hotel that covered three years of work and earned him and Keely one million dollars. Such a contract would have seemed a total fantasy just two years earlier.

The contract did allow them to stray up to a point, to do TV shows and to accept bids for one- and two-week runs at clubs. This was good publicity for the Sahara and Las Vegas in general, because if you saw "The Wildest" and wanted to see more of it, you could come to the Strip, where Louis and Keely ruled.

When they returned to the desert from a tour or the occasional vacation to visit the Prima family in New Orleans, they were welcomed with open arms. As columnist Jack Cortez reported, "The Hotel Sahara is readying the 'red carpet treatment' for the December 13th return of Louis Prima and Keely Smith, to the Casbar Lounge. In the time they've been away, the Primas vacationed at their eastern 'Pretty Acres.' However, we can't understand why they call it a vacation when they spent all of their time working. Such is the fate of a property owner."

Only a few years earlier, Prima's property had consisted of a suitcase and a used car. Now he and Keely managed to blend a love story with an old-fashioned American success story.

Louis and Keely offered a believable—and by all accounts, genuine—portrait of domestic bliss. Perhaps, entering his late forties and with a beautiful young woman who was his professional as well as personal partner, Prima was able to consistently resist his own call of the wild. One photograph from the time shows the Primas in pajamas—though they had not yet gone to sleep after the all-night shows—having breakfast at the kitchen table with Toni and their second daughter, Luanne, born in May 1957.

They maintained quite a separation between work and private life. Onstage they perpetuated the "Wildest" image, and sometimes in the Las Vegas press Louis and Keely were referred to as "Preem and Steam." But away from the Casbar Lounge, Keely was content to spend her time with her daughters. Louis was not outgoing and mostly focused on business, staying to himself even with members of the act.

"Louis was a hard man to get to know, and he could be hard to get along with," says Paul Ferrara. "Keely was sweet, but Louis . . . I don't know if it was insecurity. He had a very old-time attitude. I assume he got it from being Sicilian."

Ferrara continues: "On one hand, it was a very exciting time. You never knew who was going to be in our audience. After they split up, Jerry Lewis and Dean Martin would still come see us but just sit at opposite ends of the room. But the Chief could be tough to know. If he was sitting there with Sammy Davis or Sophia Loren or whoever, he didn't want you to sit with him. You were like a peon."

Life magazine published a profile of the couple in the summer of 1956. The piece portrayed a full night that ended at 7:00 A.M. with breakfast at home with Toni Elizabeth, who was then almost eighteen months old. Of special interest was its backstage look at Louis. In between shows from midnight to 6:00 A.M., he attended to business in the hotel's coffee shop—conferring with Barbara Belle, his business manager, setting up schedules for recording sessions, and deciding on various broadcast offers. Only when it was time to go back onstage did Prima morph into the happy-go-lucky Louis, the impresario of "The Wildest."

After breakfast, Louis and Keely went to bed. He was up by noon, and occupied the next five hours with more business matters and a round of golf, with Keely focusing on Toni. The family had dinner at five, then Louis and Keely napped until it was time to get ready to go back to work at the Sahara.

"I don't know how Louis did it, and I guess I don't know how any of us did it," Jack Carter says. "We'd be up all night, go to bed at seven, get up at ten, then go play golf all day. We got what was called Vegas throat, which is what you sound like on no sleep. All those years when I did a show at the Sahara or Riviera or Flamingo, I'd come out and croak, 'Good evening, how are you?' and people thought that was my normal speaking voice. At least I didn't have to sing, like Louis did."

In June 1957, the couple escaped the desert summer heat, but not via a vacation. They signed on to spend the summer in the more comfortable Lake Tahoe in the mountains between Reno and California. That August, producer and director Will Cowan arrived at Harrah's with a film crew to lens *The Wildest*, a short performance documentary that would end up coming the closest in Prima's career to showing his frenetic stage style.

There seemed to be an insatiable hunger for the act's albums. *The Wildest* was followed in 1957 by *Call of the Wildest*, in which Louis shared the album cover with a moose. That in turn was followed by *The Wildest Show at Tahoe*.

Another kind of work that Louis did was not onstage or in a recording studio. He knew the value of good public relations. He sent items to the reporters and columnists who covered Las Vegas entertainment for the press. One that was especially self-serving appeared in *Fabulous Las Vegas* right after Keely's much-praised appearance on television: "Keely Smith and Louis Prima 'stole the show,' when they appeared on the Dean Martin TViewer."

Louis took out print ads, even when "The Wildest" wasn't performing, such as one that ran in December 1957: "Season's Greetings. To All Our Wonderful Friends—We'll Be Seeing You Real Soon—Louis Prima * Keely Smith. Us too: Toni Elizabeth & Luanne Francis." Their second daughter's middle name was a tribute to Sinatra, which fueled some speculation about Keely's relationship with the crooner.

21

Nineteen fifty-eight would be the most successful year ever for Louis and Keely professionally. Personally, their love story was going well too, but there were indications that perhaps Keely was giving so much to the relationship as well as the act that she wasn't leaving enough for herself.

The party line since they had first met was that Louis called the shots. Keely continued to see herself as a small-town girl from Virginia who had gotten lucky with Louis, and being a headliner in Las Vegas hadn't changed that. As she told the publication *TV Reporter*, "Louis is the boss. Everybody calls him the 'Chief' [and] he's strictly boss at home and in business. It doesn't really matter to me—when a woman really loves someone then she's happy, his way."

Looking back years later at her life at that time with Louis, Keely said, "I was in love. He was my husband. That's what we did. At daytime, I stayed home with the kids and Louis went out and played golf."

To the *Los Angeles Times* in the March 1958 interview, she said, "Happiness is the key to everything. And I'm a very happy woman." Later in the article: "'I am a happy woman,' she will say over and over. 'I am happy because I enjoy my work and I love my husband.'"

And toward the end of the interview, when asked about the possibility of a solo career, she said, "One thing I know for certain, Keely Smith is nothing without Louis Prima."

One could argue that this was all she would allow herself to say for publication, but from everything Keely has said since, she probably did indeed mean every word she said. So while there was still a love story, it seemed to have become more one-sided as Louis focused on the act, related business opportunities, and apparently golf. Later, as the marriage foundered, it would be seen how the nature of the relationship almost killed Keely.

From most accounts, Louis was still a homebody, when time allowed. He had not yet bought into the swinger lifestyle made famous thanks to Frank Sinatra and his crowd.

What became known as the Rat Pack, the handful of entertainers and their entourage who would forever be identified with Las Vegas, originated in Los Angeles in the mid-1950s. The group was called the Holmby Hills Rat Pack because that is where two of the founders, Judy Garland and Sid Luft, lived, and they liked to entertain their friends, who became members and auxiliary members—Humphrey Bogart and Lauren Bacall, the leaders of the pack, and Frank Sinatra, writer Nathaniel Benchley, agent Swifty Lazar, actor David Niven, restaurateur Mike Romanoff, composer Jimmy Van Heusen, director George Cukor, and actors Spencer Tracy and Katharine Hepburn. The group was dedicated to drinking, laughing, and staying up late without caring what people said about them, and that didn't change over the years.

In the December 15, 1955, edition of the *New York Herald Tribune*, Joe Hyams wrote, "The Holmby Hills Rat Pack held its first annual meeting last night at Romanoff's restaurant in Beverly Hills and elected officers for the coming year. Named to executive positions were: Frank Sinatra, pack master; Judy Garland, first vice-president; Lauren Bacall, den mother; Humphrey Bogart, rat-in-charge-of public relations; Irving Lazar, recording secretary and treasurer."

Bogart was diagnosed with throat cancer in February 1956, and he died the following January, at age fifty-seven. Before long, Frank replaced Bogie as the head of what was called the Clan and came very close to doing the same as Bacall's husband. The home base of the group began to shift to Las Vegas.

The Strip's lore has it that the Rat Pack as a stage act began in October 1958, when, during her opening night show at the Sands, Judy Garland invited Sinatra and Dean Martin to join her onstage. They did twenty minutes of singing and joking, and the audience loved it.

Items about the Rat Pack—Sinatra changed the name from the Clan so as not to subject Sammy Davis Jr. to the obvious racial connotations—and their impromptu performances that included plenty of drinking and off-color jokes meant more space devoted to Las Vegas in the gossip columns and celebrity magazines. If you were a star seen there, it was reported everywhere. The city was the place stars were married or announced engagements, or in some cases revealed that there was a relationship.

After producer Mike Todd died, his widow, Elizabeth Taylor, was consoled by Eddie Fisher, who had been a close friend of Todd's. The fact that the friendship between Taylor and Fisher had blossomed into romance could fly under the radar in Los Angeles, for a while, anyway. But it was a different story in Nevada. Six months after Todd's death, Fisher was scheduled to begin an eight-week engagement in Las Vegas, at the Tropicana Hotel. Taylor decided to accompany him for her first public appearance since becoming a widow.

"Opening-night audiences are usually packed with friends and relatives and dedicated fans," recalled Fisher in his autobiography. "When I announced that Elizabeth was in the room that night—as if anybody hadn't noticed her entrance—the audience greeted her with affection. She was the beautiful survivor of a tragedy, the young widow left with an infant, the queen of show business. Everybody loved Elizabeth Taylor. It was a highly emotional moment for everyone in that room."

And a very public one for the couple. Fisher obtained a divorce from Debbie Reynolds and became Taylor's third husband. Only a couple of years later, he was the one being cast aside as Taylor took up with Richard Burton during the filming of Cleopatra. Fisher licked his wounds with a well-paid return to Las Vegas.

Bolstered ever further by being the head of the Rat Pack, Sinatra was viewed as the undisputed king of Las Vegas. Yet there was one person above all others he obeyed: Sam Giancana. After Al Capone was hauled off to federal prison, Giancana killed his way (it is estimated that there were two hundred notches in his leather belt) to the top of the Chicago mob. By the dawn of 1958, he rivaled Carlo Gambino of New York, the so-called boss of bosses, as the most powerful man in the American Mafia. He controlled all the numbers, prostitution, loan sharking, and other illegal pursuits in the Chicago area.

He enjoyed branching out, overseeing various crooked activities in Los Angeles, St. Louis, Miami Beach, Phoenix, and Central and South America. And, of course, Las Vegas. His points in the Riviera, Stardust, and Desert Inn meant millions of dollars of cash flowing in like a flash flood in a Nevada arroyo that didn't stop flashing. He was simply "Sam" to Sinatra, Mr. Giancana to everyone else. Because of FBI surveillance, Sinatra had to hide Giancana in the Sands when the mobster visited Vegas.

Frank and Sam were good friends who enjoyed partying together and sleeping with some of the same women, and they benefited each other. It was no secret that Sinatra was under Giancana's protection, so he was untouchable everywhere he went. Giancana liked the cachet of having the country's biggest star at his side or a phone call away. The only person Frank really had to fear was Sam himself. If he refused a request to perform (sometimes gratis) at one of Giancana's clubs, or tried to sleep with one of the boss's women without permission, or was even thought to be talking to law enforcement at any level, Sinatra knew he was a dead man.

Unlike during the days of the Famous Door in New York, there apparently are no stories floating around of connections between Louis and Keely and the mob in Las Vegas. As a mostly stay-at-home mom offstage, Keely stayed somewhat isolated. Surely Louis rubbed up against mobsters who had financial interests in the Sahara or were simply patrons in the lounge. But it seems that he was unaffected by their presence.

"The Wildest" probably performed at private parties for top Mafia men, perhaps because of their friendship with Sinatra and the mobsters behind Milton Prell, and it was a smart thing not to say no or cause trouble. (Everyone on the Strip knew the story of how Joe E. Lewis had had his throat cut in 1927 by Jack "Machine Gun" McGurn, an Al Capone lieutenant, for refusing to sign a contract with a Capone nightclub.) Otherwise, though, Louis and his band went about their business, not needing the mob to get them gigs or make them more famous. The Sicilian heritage that he and Sam Butera shared aided them among the gangsters, but for the most part the act had a life of its own by then, and among American audiences it was about to become much bigger.

Debbie Reynolds bounced back from her breakup with Eddie Fisher to become an even more favored star as an actress during the next few years—*How the West Was Won* and *The Unsinkable Molly Brown* were hits at the box office—and as a stage act. With the latter, she learned a lot from watching the performers in Las Vegas. With and without Fisher, she ran with the Rat Pack along the Strip. One of her favorite shows was Louis Prima and Keely Smith.

"Everybody after work went to hang out where Louis and Keely were," Reynolds remembers. "No matter what hotel you were booked into, the Sands was the first place to go because of Sammy Davis Jr., Dean Martin, and of course Frank, and then it was time to hit the Casbar Lounge to see Louis and Keely. They were just incredible performers, and Sam and the band seemed to have more energy than anyone else, and this was at four and five in the morning."

Reynolds became good friends with the couple offstage, and the many shows of theirs she saw and her talent for mimicry would result in a big favor for Louis a few years later.

The pace of performing six shows a week until dawn and caring for two daughters, recording in the studio, and taking side trips for lucrative gigs elsewhere—without the expediency of quick journeys because of Louis's fear of flying—as well as what was becoming an emotionally one-sided relationship with her husband all took their toll on Keely. (In the 1970 interview, Louis claimed he did not fear flying but that "the plane doesn't move once it's in the air. That's why I prefer to travel by train, because I can feel it going someplace.")

In late March 1958, while onstage in the Casbar Lounge, she almost fainted and couldn't finish the show. The next day she traveled to Los Angeles to be admitted to Cedars of Lebanon Hospital. "Presumably, to undergo minor surgery," the *Las Vegas Review-Journal* speculated in the absence of any other information.

But when Keely was released, the pace continued. The *New York Times* reported on May 22, "Louis Prima and Keely Smith and their musical group known as the Witnesses will appear regularly on Milton Berle's new television show in the fall." (This was premature, as Prima and Berle got into an acrimonious spat over the financial terms of the contract that kept the gossip columnists busy for a while.) Two days earlier, "The Wildest" had returned to the Sahara for a new run, replacing the Mary Kaye Trio, which wound its way north to Harrah's in Reno.

Louis and Keely were now recording almost constantly, putting more strain on her. When he had first made the deal with Capitol Records in 1956, Louis was already thinking ahead to helping Keely embark on a solo recording career.

"When Capitol Records came along, and we were at the Sahara and we had gotten so hot, they wanted to sign the group, and Louis said, 'OK, but you have to give Keely her own individual contract,'" she recalled years later in an interview. "Their response was no. So Louis said, 'Well, then you can't have the group.' About two months later they came back and said, 'OK, we'll take her.'"

Given that Louis had a large ego, was a self-promoter, and had to be the Chief, one might wonder why Keely as a solo act was important to him. Allowing him some credit, Louis loved his wife and was impressed by her talent. Just as likely, if not more likely, was that this was another challenge for the restless bandleader, and any success that Keely encountered would reflect well on him.

When the time came to make her first album, in November 1957, Keely and Louis and Voyle Gilmore, the executive who had signed them, began choosing songs. Gilmore called one of them a "pretty song" but doubted it would be a hit: "I Wish You Love." It had been written as "Que Reste-til de Nos Amours" by the French composer Charles Trenet in 1955.

After listening to it, Keely told Louis, "Babe, I'll do any eleven songs y'all want, but let me sing the French song."

Gilmore said, "Well, that's not going to amount to anything. That's just a pretty song."

"Man, if she wants to sing the French song," Louis declared, "she's going to sing the French song."

She did. It became the title track of her debut album, which was arranged by Nelson Riddle, who had been lent to Louis and Keely by Sinatra. In the Grammy Awards for 1958, Keely was nominated in the Best Female Vocal category for that song, which had been a national hit. She lost out to the singer who had been one of her two favorites to listen to on the radio back in Norfolk, Ella Fitzgerald.

Also featured on the disc were "Fools Rush In," "When Your Lover Has Gone," and "When Day Is Done." She said, "Every one of those arrangements is a Nelson Riddle arrangement. That is not a normal procedure for Louis Prima. He always had say-so over everything. But I think because Nelson was Sinatra's arranger, Louis decided not to try to tell this man what to do, just go ahead and write. Those ideas came from his head, not Louis's."

When the album was released in 1958, John S. Wilson wrote in the *New York Times*: "Keely Smith, whose long career as the stone-faced stooge in Louis Prima's raucous troupe has brought her close to the fringes of jazz, turns away from both stooging and jazz on *I Wish You Love* (Capitol) to sing a set of love songs with hitherto unsuspected warmth and sensitivity. Miss Smith is not yet an assured singer in this area but she gives evidence on this disk that she could be an unusually good ballad singer. She is helped greatly by the understanding, graceful arrangements of Nelson Riddle."

For the first time since the late 1930s, Prima went in front of movie cameras. He and Keely made a film that year titled *Senior Prom*, directed by David Lowell Rich, that also featured Butera and the Witnesses and a cast of mostly young, unknown actors including Tom Laughlin, who in the 1970s would go on to star in and direct the popular Billy Jack series of films.

"*Senior Prom* is another of those musical salads of the 1950s, heavy on the guest stars but very light on plot," was a typical review. Sharing the screen with Louis and Keely to do musical numbers were Bob Crosby, Freddy Martin and His Orchestra, Les Elgart, and Mitch Miller. Even Ed Sullivan made an appearance. An interesting tidbit about the movie was that the associate producer was Moe Howard, reuniting with Louis after the Three Stooges had performed with Louis's orchestra in New York in the 1940s.

Another film was announced in the trade press, *Bourbon Street Blues*, that would star Louis, but it was not produced. (There is now a nightclub with that name in New Orleans.)

"The Wildest" had done such a fine job of putting the Casbar Lounge on the national map that it became a good career move to play there and be associated in any way with the act.

"Louis might have been the most successful lounge performer in Vegas history," recalled Don Rickles (in *Rickles' Book*), who entertained the crowd in the Casbar with his emerging insult humor when Louis and Keely and the band took breaks. "With singer Keely Smith looking sultry and seductive, with his backup band Sam Butera and the Witnesses blowing their brains out, Louis rocked and rolled every night of the week. He sang, he joked, he carried on until the audience was exhausted. Every night I asked myself: How can I follow this guy?"

In his autobiography, written with David Ritz, the comic remembered, "The setup was strange. Right in front of the stage was a pit where the waiters and bartenders walked back and forth serving food and drinks. . . . At the 5 A.M. show, if I saw that the lounge was empty, I ran offstage, ran into the casino, stood by one of the crap tables and yelled, 'Hold down the noise! I'm trying to do a show in there!' Then I ran back into the Casbar with a new following of fans eager to see what this nut case was screaming about."

Rickles recalled one particular young comic sitting at one of the lounge's tables after his own act was done. "Hey, Rickles, when's Louis Prima coming out?" Johnny Carson asked repeatedly. Beginning in 1962, when Carson became the host of *The Tonight Show*, he would showcase many of the Las Vegas acts that he had admired as he was cutting his comedic teeth there in the 1950s.

It was during 1958 that Keely and Frank Sinatra first collaborated in a recording studio. "Nothing in Common" was a duet done for Capitol, and it would be Sinatra's last commercially issued 78-RPM record.

"Louis drove me to Capitol Records, handed me over to Frank, and took a train to New Orleans," Keely remembered. "He left me—who didn't know my ass from a hole in the ground in those days—with Frank Sinatra. Everyone thought we were having a big romance. We didn't, but I could kick myself now."

The song was written by Rat Packers Sammy Cahn and Jimmy Van Heusen. Keely and Frank had a brief discussion, and then they did a take. "OK, that one's good," said Frank in his customary way—as with making movies, he didn't like doing more than one take.

But it hadn't sounded quite right to Keely, and she was used to Prima's more rigorous recording sessions. "No, no, that's not good," she announced. "I think we can do better."

There was shocked silence in the studio. Everyone braced for an explosion. One did not disagree with Sinatra, especially when it came to his music. Frank grinned and said, "You're right. Let's do it again." The second take ended up on the album.

When Louis and Keely next stepped into the studio, it was not to record an album but a single, "That Old Black Magic." Louis had first recorded it as a duet with Lily Ann Carol. She was only sixteen when she joined his orchestra in 1939, and she stayed with the Gleeby Rhythm Orchestra through World War II. After several others had recorded or at least performed the 1942 tune, she and Prima incorporated it into the act. That had ended when Carol left the orchestra in 1946.

Apparently, Prima had filed the song away and waited for an opportunity to try it out again. In Keely, he had the best singer to do a duet with. Sammy Davis Jr. had recorded and released a version in 1955 that did well, so Louis had to bide his time. In 1958, he was ready. "That Old Black Magic" was recorded not as part of an album but as a stand-alone single.

It immediately received airplay and jumped onto the Top 40 charts, where it remained for two months. Among the audiences who crowded into the smoky and sometimes stifling Casbar Lounge, it became the couple's most requested song, and it was the same with Ed Sullivan and other TV hosts.

Louis and Keely had risen to the pinnacle of their popularity, and with the exception of Sinatra no act was more in demand in Las Vegas—well, certainly after 3:00 A.M. The last four years had indeed been magical.

ACT III

I Wish You Love

22

Keely's debut album had been so successful and her popularity as a singer rose so rapidly that the executives at Capitol Records did a complete reversal and were now eager for her to record as a solo artist. Apparently Louis did not feel threatened by this development, at least not initially. With his big ego intact, it may never have occurred to him that his wife could actually eclipse him as a figure in the music business—though there is a somewhat defensive hint to the title of an album that he would record and issue in 1959: *Strictly Prima*. And there was a financial incentive: he viewed Keely's achievements as allowing them both to keep riding the wave of escalating performing fees and recording royalties.

"Everything was working well, every song was a hit for Keely, everything that Louis did and everything that Louis and Keely did was a big success," said Joe Segreto in the documentary *Louis Prima: The Wildest!* about 1958, when the couple reached the height of their fame. "They were doing a lot of television at the time, when television was really taking off."

As far as the public and the people who knew them could tell, Louis was genuinely proud of his wife's success. There was, of course, ego involved here too, because he and Keely were the Las Vegas version of Henry Higgins and Eliza Doolittle, and everything she had gained in her life she owed to him.

What she achieved satisfied Louis's burning desire to be more famous and more successful.

"Louis was so ambitious it was unreal," Sam Butera stated in the 1983 TV documentary *Louis Prima—The Chief* (which offers glimpses of first wife Louise and daughter Joyce attending a 1981 tribute to Prima in New Orleans). "It was uncanny the way he would get what he wanted. He planned it all out. Even in the car, we'd be driving to a show; he'd turn off the radio and say, 'Leave me alone,' so no one would interfere with his thinking."

Keely was back in the studio in June 1958 to create a follow-up to *I Wish You Love.* She worked with arranger Billy May, another Sinatra collaborator, on *Politely,* which included the tunes "The Song Is You," "I Can't Get Started," "On the Sunny Side of the Street," and "I'll Never Smile Again." It too sold well, so before the end of the year Keely was recording "It's Magic," "Stardust," "Stormy Weather," "Someone to Watch Over Me," and other classics (or about to be) for the album *Swinging Pretty,* with Nelson Riddle back as the arranger.

"The procedure for selecting the tracks on these albums was simple," critic Joseph F. Laredo wrote. "Standards and the pop tunes of the day were tried out in live performance first, and those that elicited the most gratifying audience reaction made it into the lineup."

Keely was doing double duty because she and Louis and Sam Butera and the Witnesses continued to record as "The Wildest" to fulfill the Capitol contract and the nearly insatiable demand of the public. And then Hollywood came calling.

As a teenager in Virginia, Dottie Smith might have dreamed of being in a Hollywood movie with a famous and handsome male lead, but she would not have expected it to really happen. And like many young women in the late 1940s, one of the actors she fancied was Robert Mitchum. Now, because of Mitchum, Keely was about to make a big step up from such film fare as *Senior Prom.*

By 1958, Mitchum was one of the most popular actors in the world. He had gotten noticed in such 1940s film noir classics as *Out of the Past,* and in the '50s was loved by the (mostly female) audience in box office hits like *River of No Return* with Marilyn Monroe and by critics in *Night of the Hunter.* He was branching out to producing some of his own pictures, and his latest project was *Thunder Road.*

Mitchum played Korean War veteran Lucas Doolin, who drives fast and hard through the mountains of Kentucky and Tennessee as the fearless delivery man of the family's moonshine business. He is targeted by both government agents and a gangster who wants his organization to take control of all the independent moonshine makers. Doolin doesn't want his younger brother to follow in his footsteps. For romance, when Doolin is in town he dallies with Francie Wymore, a nightclub singer.

James Agee—known for the book *Let Us Now Praise Famous Men* and who years before had cowritten the film *The African Queen*—knew a story about a fast-driving moonshiner who had died in a crash. He passed it along to Mitchum, who decided to produce it as a film. Mitchum also cowrote the script and the music and reportedly directed much of the film himself, though Arthur Ripley received the credit. Mitchum handed the script to Elvis Presley to play Robin, the younger brother. Presley was ready to sign on, but his manager, Col. Tom Parker, demanded too much money, so the role went to James Mitchum, Robert's sixteen-year-old son. In March 1957, the elder Mitchum had released an album of songs titled *Calypso—Is Like So* . . . He was a music aficionado and a fan of "The Wildest." For the role of Francie, he turned to a fellow Capitol recording artist, Keely Smith.

While Louis may have been uncomfortable (or worse) with the love scenes between his wife and Mitchum, Keely could only have done the picture with Louis's permission. Everything she did professionally depended on her husband's approval. She told *Newsweek* magazine in June 1958, three months after the *Los Angeles Times* interview, that anything new that happened to her was entirely due to "God, luck, and Louis Prima," and added, "I don't think I'll ever do anything unless Louis OKs it or supervises it or directs it."

Thunder Road went straight to box-office gold after it was released on May 10, 1958. It was a big favorite of the drive-in crowd and has attained cult movie status. "Whippoorwill," a song from the film, cowritten for Keely by Mitchum, was a hit, as was Mitchum's own "The Ballad of Thunder Road." (In 1975, there was another successful song, written by Bruce Springsteen, that was titled "Thunder Road" and was inspired by the movie.) For Keely, her first foray as a featured actress in a Hollywood movie was boffo, which in turn made "The Wildest" an even bigger attraction among Las Vegas tourists and television audiences.

Still, Keely maintained about the time, "I didn't know how big we were. That didn't matter to me. I was just very happy being with Louis, being with my kids, and singing or whatever."

It wasn't easy trying to be family people between the traveling and the demands of the lounge act. Prima's lifelong fear of flying meant trips to New York for concerts and TV shows and anywhere in the United States to fulfill bookings took longer. And wherever they went, they were on a tether because they always had to return to the Casbar Lounge. They were yet to grow tired of it; instead they relished it.

"I just think the lounge made us work harder," Keely told Mike Weatherford in *Cult Vegas*. "It kept our feet on the ground. When you're all over the country with first-class treatment in the best hotels, it's kind of hard to keep your feet on the ground. If you're in Las Vegas working midnight til six in the morning, and your best friends are cab drivers and hookers and waitresses, you're pretty normal."

"I had two beautiful daughters," Keely reminisced to *Port Folio Weekly* in September 2003. "In the daytime I would stay home with them, and Louis would go play golf, and in the night time we would go to work. So it didn't dawn on me that we were stars or not stars."

That Louis went out almost every day to play golf with the boys didn't mean that he was becoming a more gregarious man. He was passionate about golf, and there had to be a foursome to go out on the course, and that was as far as it went.

"His whole thing was 'familiarity breeds contempt,' that's how he lived his life," Sam Butera said about Prima. "We played golf and he said, 'I'll see you later, Sam, see you at the job tonight.' But on stage, he made me laugh, listening to him and the way he did things and the way he moved. Nobody could mess with him. Frank Sinatra came on stage, Dean Martin came on stage, Jerry Lewis—no matter who, they could not mess with Louis Prima. He had a certain way. He laughed at them, and the people were looking at him instead of looking at them."

23

___

As in the rest of America, there were changes brewing in Las Vegas in the twilight of the 1950s. The Dwight Eisenhower administration was in its last couple of years. The launch of satellites by the Soviet Union and the United States had initiated a space race. Rock 'n' roll songs and especially Elvis Presley tunes were being played on more radio stations. In the South, lunch counter boycotts and other civil rights protests endeavored to change long-held practices and prejudices.

A particularly significant change in Las Vegas was that the offstage barriers to black performers were weakening and soon to come down. A march of protest along the Strip took place in 1958, and among the marchers were Lena Horne, Pearl Bailey, and Marlene Dietrich. They and other black performers refused to sign contracts with hotels that would not make all facilities available to them. Sinatra was fed up that Sammy Davis Jr. couldn't stay at the Sands, and he boycotted the hotel—even though he owned a percentage of it and was its biggest draw—until that door swung open.

"The growing clout of the entertainers had much to do with ending segregation abruptly," wrote Mike Weatherford in *Cult Vegas* about what would happen when the new decade began. "Three years prior, Harry Belafonte had negotiated a written contract with the Riviera that guaranteed the headliner's suite. Billy Eckstine had more direct methods, according to Claude

145

Trenier. When a dice-table stick man informed him, 'We don't let niggers play here,' Eckstine cold-cocked him."

The Grammy Awards ceremony held in 1959 was a triumph for Louis and Keely. Best Vocal Performance by a Duo or Group formed a Grammy category for the first time, and they won that award for "That Old Black Magic." (For the fiftieth anniversary of the song, Keely went onstage at the 2008 Grammy Awards to sing some of the song, with Kid Rock replacing Prima as her sidekick.)

The Grammys ceremony should have been a triumph for their friend Frank Sinatra too. With Nelson Riddle the previous year, he had recorded two of the finest albums of his career, *Only the Lonely* and *Come Fly with Me*, the two bestselling discs of 1958. *Only the Lonely* went to number one, and it remained on the bestseller charts for over two years. It continues to be one of his truly great albums, and how fitting (and anticipated) it would have been for Sinatra to receive the Best Male Vocal award. But the winner was Domenico Modugno for the song "Volare," and the Best Album award went to Henry Mancini's *The Music from Peter Gunn*, based on the TV show. Frank was furious over one of the very few times at this point in his life when he didn't get his way.

There were indications that, by taking full advantage of their popularity, Louis and Keely were becoming overextended. *Variety* reported in March 1959 that in Hollywood a producer, Irving Levin, filed a breach of contract lawsuit against them, for just over two thousand dollars, for backing out of a deal to film a pilot for a TV series they had intended to do. The paltry amount implies the suit was more out of pique than anything else, or it could have been a small-time shakedown, but it was not unlikely that there were offers on the table for a "Wildest"-related television show.

Making sure that when Keely made another movie he would be the leading man, Louis explored combining film and recording efforts. "It's understood that Prima has been dickering with other labels, among them MGM and Dot, for a new tie when his pact with Capitol runs out," *Variety* reported in April. It went on to say that Louis was "looking for a disk affiliation with a built-in motion picture company tie because he's scouting a simultaneous indie producer setup. Dot is tied to Paramount and MGM is aligned with the Metro studio."

Another sign of cracks in the act was that, for the first time, Louis's health failed him. That spring he experienced dizziness and headaches. Initially, he blamed his feelings on sagebrush and mesquite pollen in the surrounding area and the clouds of cigarette smoke in the Casbar Lounge. He even cast some blame on his trumpet, thinking it might contain dust or bacteria. The band took a hiatus, and Louis went to the hospital for two operations, which seems odd as a response to allergic reactions. Being ever-private offstage, no information was given out about the operations.

However, most odd is that, in a statement he did issue to the press, Louis offered that while he was in the hospital "rumors were started that Keely and I were breaking up. This is a preposterous lie, started by some imbecile. We have a wonderful family life, and we have two beautiful children, and Keely and I love each other very much." He insisted that rumors that they would not be returning to the Casbar Lounge were untrue and that "it will be wonderful seeing you all again."

They were welcomed back with open arms by tourists and celebrities alike. "They were *the* act to see in the late hours," recalls Connie Stevens, who was just emerging as a singer and actress in the late '50s. "There were a lot of laughs and it was exhausting, but for me it was more fun than I'd ever had."

Las Vegas was becoming even more of a playground for the famous, and the rest of the country paid increasing attention. The gossip columnists had almost more material than they had space to report celebrity happenings.

"The Tropicana engagement was my first major live appearance since the scandal became public, and I really did not know how the audience was going to respond to me," recalled Eddie Fisher about the headlines that followed his split with Debbie Reynolds and his relationship with Elizabeth Taylor. "Because Elizabeth was going to be there, the media descended on Vegas. . . . I was quite nervous when I walked out onstage opening night, until I looked down and saw Elizabeth smiling at me. 'I opened here two years ago,' I began. 'Since then, nothing much has happened.' The audience laughed, maybe even a little louder and longer than the joke was worth, but it was their way of letting me know they were with me."

But most of the headlines were devoted to Sinatra and his pals, who were soon to become more visible on the big screen. What could be considered the first Rat Pack movie was, strangely, not shot in Las Vegas but in Indiana. Sinatra had signed on to star in *Some Came Running*, James Jones's follow-up bestseller to *From Here to Eternity*. He played a heavy-drinking, gambling, would-be writer who returns to his Midwestern hometown after a long absence that included being in the Army. The second male lead was also a heavy drinker and gambler. Who else but Dean Martin for the part? And for the nice girl who falls for the star: Shirley MacLaine.

But they imported their Las Vegas lifestyle to the Midwest. "We were on our movie location in Madison, Indiana, when The Boys from Chicago visited Frank," MacLaine recalled in *My Lucky Stars*, referring to men sent by Giancana to observe the film's shooting. "I didn't know who they were. I only knew that the nightlife of poker, jokes, pasta, and booze went on until five A.M. Our calls were at six A.M."

Soon one of "The Boys" was Giancana himself. MacLaine would learn more about what he was really like some years later in Mexico City. She was shooting *Two Mules for Sister Sara* with Clint Eastwood and on a day off went to see Sammy Davis Jr. perform at a nightclub. When she went backstage looking for Sammy, Giancana was there.

The mob boss kept insisting that she have some pasta, and each time she refused he twisted her arm behind her back harder. Davis came out of his dressing room and saw that Shirley was in pain. He intervened, and Giancana slugged him in the stomach. "OK, no pasta for you either," he said.

Without help from mobsters, Louis and Keely went back before the movie cameras. For better or worse, the definitive Prima-Smith movie is *Hey Boy! Hey Girl!*, which was released in March 1959. Also opening on the big screen that week were *All Mine to Give* with Cameron Mitchell and Glynis Johns, *The Violators* with Arthur O'Connell, *The Big Fisherman* featuring Howard Keel, *It Happened to Jane* with Doris Day and Jack Lemmon, *The Scapegoat* starring Alec Guinness, *Scampolo* with European temptress Romy Schneider, and an Alfred Hitchcock classic, *North by Northwest*, starring Cary Grant, Eva Marie Saint, and James Mason.

Hey Boy! Hey Girl! is certainly no classic musical of the 1950s, but it has some enjoyable scenes and is the best feature-length representation on the big screen of the Prima-Smith-Butera dynamic, though the plot is far from being the "wildest." It's a low-budget showcase from Columbia Pictures that also features a recognizable supporting actor, James Gregory. It took only eleven days to shoot the movie late in 1958, nine of them in Las Vegas.

Keely plays Dorothy Spencer, who is trying to raise funds for her church's youth camp. She approaches Louis at the club where he is performing, and he is first seen singing "Oh Marie," backed by Sam and the Witnesses, who are also playing themselves. Louis agrees to help the youth camp, and that effort is interspersed with modestly romantic scenes as the two fall in love, accompanied by some finger-snapping musical numbers.

While not anywhere near the Top 10, the film did well at the box office, just one more indication that there was a substantial audience for anything the couple did. Keely exhibited an assured screen presence, and Columbia Pictures gave it a strong promotional push. One advertisement blared, "Smash Capitol Records promotion of soundtrack album! Socko standee displays in 8,000 record stores! Saturation deejay coverage!"

Despite such cooperation from the company, Prima decided that he and his wife would leave Capitol Records. As a couple and, for Keely, as a solo act, they had enjoyed a lot of success with the label, and an "if it ain't broke don't fix it" attitude might have been wiser. But Dot Records, which had Pat Boone and Debbie Reynolds in its stable, stepped in with a substantial advance and offered that Prima would keep control of the masters they recorded, which could mean millions as years passed. If the couple continued at the rate of success they were enjoying, this one contract would set them up financially for the rest of their lives.

Louis and Keely would certainly be industrious in the recording studio, creating and releasing eight albums in just over two years, including twenty-five singles. In 1960, they released one of their most enduring albums sales-wise, *Louis and Keely!* It featured the couple's versions of "Night and Day," "I'm Confessin' (That I Love You)," "Make Love to Me," and "Cheek to Cheek" among the twelve tracks.

However, they were not a good fit at Dot (despite its being her childhood name), and, as Keely later commented, "It was never the same after that, not like it had been at Capitol."

They ended what was to date their most successful year with a smash show. They opened at the Moulin Rouge in Hollywood on New Year's Eve, 1958. Twelve hundred people were turned away that night. It was estimated that during Louis and Keely's seven-day engagement, fifteen thousand would-be audience members couldn't obtain seats. Even at the height of his fame as a bandleader, Prima alone could not have done such business.

24

Louis kept his Italian roots close and performed some of the novelty songs from early in his career even in the arid, neon landscape of Nevada. "Oh Marie" was a regular in the act, and he sang it almost entirely in Italian dialect. As George Guida describes it in his *Journal of Popular Culture* article, "Dancing and clapping, he pours every ounce of energy into performing an Italian troubador's song for the unflappable Smith, who stands by impassively and watches, like a Mardi Gras debutante. Such an *Americana* is not easily won, so Prima enlists the help of his own krewe, his own tribe, the band. The persona of the song swears to his love, 'Sona chitarra mia!' ('My guitar plays for you!'), so Prima pleads with Butera to play HIS instrument, the saxophone. Butera steps forward for 'una nota,' which he cannot deliver for laughing. Prima notices and quips, 'What's the matter, Sam? You can't play in Italian?'"

With the exception of their appearances on Ed Sullivan's show, the most popular television exposure "The Wildest" ever received was on April 5, 1959, a Sunday, on *The Dinah Shore Chevy Show*, one of the small screen's most-watched programs. The timing was perfect: *Hey Boy! Hey Girl!*, the movie headlined by the couple, was in theaters, and it was the five hundredth broadcast of Shore's show and thus heavily hyped in print ads.

Louis, Keely, Sam, and the band were onscreen for the first fifteen minutes of the show. Their first number was, predictably, "When You're Smiling."

According to David Kamp in a detailed *Vanity Fair* article published forty years later, after a new viewing of the Shore show:

> Prima, an apelike 48-year-old man dressed in a dark blazer and white slacks, is a dervish of caffeinated motion—dancing and leaping maniacally as he sings, tugging up his pant legs to reveal his pale hosiery and happy feet, waving his trumpet around like a flyswatter when he's not bleating urgent, staccato notes through it.
>
> His sidemen are equally frenetic. Butera, squatter and younger, weaves in and out of Prima's path, grinning orgasmically, swinging his tenor sax between his legs to flagrant phallic effect. The Witnesses, five pomaded young men in matching dinner jackets, shout backing vocals, snap their fingers, and shimmy like hopped-up Jets out of *West Side Story.*
>
> Amid all the commotion, the lovely Keely Smith, in a poufed white ball gown, stands stock-still back by the piano, voicing her 'When you're smiling's' with a flat, vaguely peeved expression, as if her galoot boyfriend strong-armed her into spending their postprom hours with his greaseball friends who quit school and work at the car wash.

As Kamp's piece indicates, what the American audience saw that night was a big reason why "The Wildest" was such a hoot: sex. They were, after all, from Las Vegas and thus did not have to abide by the same standards as the rest of the country.

They perform two songs by Jule Styne and Sammy Cahn, "It's Magic" and "It's Been a Long, Long Time," then comes "Louis and Keely's consummation of their unlikely love on 'That Old Black Magic,' performed by the Witnesses as a breakneck rumba," Kamp continued.

As the song goes on and the couple trade lines, "The ice melts. Keely, getting into it now, mugs cross-eyed and sends up Louis's ape-man gesticulations, galumphing across the stage with her jaw slackened and her arms swinging; he mimics her compulsive nose-scratching, pawing his proboscis every time she itches hers. She beams at him adoringly. He jumps up and down a few more times."

Kamp concludes, "It's unlikely, in 1959, that anyone has ever seen a more entertaining, or frankly libidinous, quarter-hour of television."

But still not as risqué as their live performances in Las Vegas. During one of the "Wildest" shows at the Desert Inn, Keely said to the audience, "Doesn't he look like the Indian on the nickel? I wish he was the buffalo." Louis offered, "Once she gets home, she's dead, believe me." Keely responded, "That's the only way we can start even. Believe me."

The audience thought the racy repartee was hilarious. No one knew that the trouble brewing between them did have to do in large part with sex, but it wasn't that Louis couldn't perform. This bubbled below the surface for the time being, with just the occasional hint that Prima was re-establishing a pattern of cheating on his wife.

Surely, most people thought, it had to be different with Keely. The fourth wife was the special one. They were living a love story most American couples could only dream about. Never chatty with the press, unless it served a direct PR purpose, Louis became even more reluctant to do interviews. He claimed that he had nothing to say about himself, and he was interesting only because of what he did during shows.

As his brother, Leon, said about Louis: "His life was onstage. That's what he wanted, to always be onstage."

When Dinah Shore introduced "The Wildest" on her show, she called them "the greatest nightclub act in the country. They're knocking 'em dead in Las Vegas." But there was one act in town that continued to prevent Louis and Keely from claiming that their act was indeed the greatest—Frank Sinatra, now surrounded by the Rat Pack, whose throne was at the Sands.

As individual performers, Sinatra, Dean Martin, Sammy Davis Jr., and Joey Bishop were favorites among Las Vegas audiences, and of course Sinatra was arguably the most popular entertainer in the country. But more often they began to take to the stage together, with lightweight song-and-dance man Peter Lawford in tow (Sinatra favored him because he was related by marriage to John F. Kennedy), and as a group they were idolized by the tourists, who believed they were experiencing a very special kind of entertainment.

In early 1960, casino boss Jack Entratter nicknamed these occasions the Summit after the meeting set for that spring between the leaders of France,

Great Britain, the Soviet Union, and the United States. In the four weeks that Sinatra and his pals played the hotel that first time officially, during a movie shoot in Las Vegas, scalpers collected up to a hundred dollars each for three-dollar tickets.

According to Nancy Sinatra, "When they worked together, it was a summit meeting indeed, a gathering—within the entertainment world—of the top. Frank and Dean and Sammy. Joey Bishop. Peter Lawford. And whoever else from the upper ranks of show business—Bing Crosby, Milton Berle, Don Rickles, Judy Garland, Shirley MacLaine—happened to be around at that time and in that place."

The unquestioned leader of the pack was Old Blue Eyes. Despite a schedule that put even Louis and Keely to shame, Sinatra kept producing in the recording studio and in front of cameras at a very high level. In the three years that concluded the 1950s, he recorded 124 songs in thirty-seven recording sessions, with many of those songs being the best in the Sinatra catalogue. He made six feature films: *The Pride and the Passion*, *The Joker Is Wild*, *Pal Joey*, *Kings Go Forth*, *Some Came Running*, and *A Hole in the Head*. He also had a steady diet of concerts and appeared on over three dozen TV shows. And it was always a major event when he took to a stage in Las Vegas. Several estimates contended that he earned more money than anyone in the history of show business, and this was without factoring in what he received under the table and the gambling credit the mobster owners granted him.

"When we got together and made pictures at the same time that the Clan was appearing in Vegas, there was an energy there that has never been duplicated since," according to Shirley MacLaine. "Two shows a night, seven days a week, for three months . . . while shooting a picture. Granted, these pictures were not award winners, . . . but the spontaneous humor on the stage and the set was unparalleled then and has never been matched since."

Powered by Sinatra's still-increasing fame, the Sands Hotel had become the place to be, and would remain so for years to come. In *Play It as It Lays* by Joan Didion, there is this passage:

Maria sat on a couch in the ladies' room of the Flamingo with the attendant and a Cuban who was killing the hour between her ten o'clock and midnight dates and she knew that she could not go back out to the crap tables.

"Like a cemetery," the Cuban said.

The attendant shrugged. "Every place the same."

"Not the Sands, I could hardly get through the Sands tonight."

The Sands was glad to take full advantage of the growing Rat Pack legend. A marquee in January 1960 listed Frank Sinatra, Dean Martin, Sammy Davis Jr.—actually, in an advertisement it was "The Will Mastin Trio starring Sammy Davis Jr."—Peter Lawford, and Joey Bishop. They wouldn't necessarily all be onstage that night, but it was promoted that, because all were in Las Vegas filming *Ocean's Eleven*, two or perhaps more would be part of any night's show.

The group even had nicknamed white bathrobes. Sinatra's read "Pope," Martin's said "Dago," Davis had "Smokey" embroidered on his (and he had the only brown robe), and on and on. They were on a path to creating their own offhand language to communicate among themselves: women were "broads," God was the "big G," death was the "big casino," a penis was a "bird," sex was a "little hey-hey" (which is what Sinatra proposes to Angie Dickinson in *Ocean's Eleven*), and "dullsville" pretty much applied to anyplace that wasn't as fun and freewheeling as Las Vegas.

That *Ocean's Eleven* is a pretty enjoyable movie is something of a miracle considering the chaos that surrounded shooting it. Actually, the project was born in chaos—in 1958, an entire raft of writers cobbled together a script about eleven men who served together in the 82nd Airborne reuniting to rob five casinos in Las Vegas. Quite a while later, once a final script was approved, the Warner Bros. project was given to Lewis Milestone to produce and direct.

Milestone had made the classic film adaptation of *All Quiet on the Western Front*, but that had been in 1930, and at sixty-four he wasn't up to the task of corralling the Rat Pack. Sinatra's Dorchester Productions was also on board as a producer, so he was the director's boss as well as the star. Of course, filming took place at the Sands. During the weeks of shooting, the members of the Rat Pack played all night then staggered to the various locations in the morning.

The film began lensing on January 26, and the crew wrapped up their work in Las Vegas on February 16. It was a Rat Pack marathon of insults and seltzer-squirting interrupted by the occasional song at the Sands every night after shooting ended—or, more accurately, after Sinatra decided that there had been enough filming for one day.

The movie opened in August 1960 to mediocre reviews, but the Rat Pack was hot, and it did well at the box office. A celebrity-filled crowd showed up when *Ocean's Eleven* was first shown at the Fremont Theatre after a show Sinatra and friends performed at the Sands.

Few remembered that *Ocean's Eleven* was actually the second movie shot at the Sands. *Meet Me in Las Vegas*, a pleasing MGM musical, had been released in 1956. Ballet dancer Cyd Charisse visits Vegas and brings good luck to local rancher Dan Dailey. Also on hand to provide music are Lena Horne, Sammy Davis Jr., and Frankie Laine.

Louis Prima and Keely Smith make an appearance in *Ocean's Eleven* too—but only as names listed along with Donald O'Connor in a shot that shows the Sahara marquee.

25

Given the relatively small population of Nevada and the fact that Las Vegas was a place to play, where only the money was serious, the town would not necessarily be considered significant in national politics. But that was about to change too, because of the vast amount of money on the Strip and that money's intersection with a future president who already knew quite a bit about playing with celebrities. Among John F. Kennedy's favorite songs was the Louis and Keely version of "That Old Black Magic," and if they were onstage and JFK was in town, the senator from Massachusetts could be found in the audience.

Sinatra was already a Kennedy connection in Los Angeles and Las Vegas, but the connection became a bond when the singer took the senator's brother-in-law Peter Lawford under his wing. Sinatra had attended the 1956 Democratic convention. When Adlai Stevenson received the nomination to run again against Dwight Eisenhower—JFK's wife, Jackie, wrote the endorsement speech for him—Bobby Kennedy declared that the family should begin to plan for the 1960 race immediately. Sinatra volunteered to be part of that effort.

It included raising lots of cash, sometimes in unconventional ways, and giving it to the Kennedy campaign. Over the years, JFK increasingly enjoyed

Las Vegas—being a guest member of the Clan/Summit/Rat Pack, the women, and the cash that would underwrite his campaign for the White House.

"Whenever J.F.K. or another person of prominence sat in the audience, Dad gave a colleague the honor of introducing him or her to the crowd," recalled Nancy Sinatra. "One time Dean Martin would do it, another time Sammy, and so on. I remember the night Dean said to a room that was full of extra excitement and some kind of tangible glow: 'There's a senator here tonight and this senator is running for President or something and we play golf together, we go fishing together, and he's one of my best buddies' and he turned to FS and said, 'What the hell *is* his name?' and John Kennedy started laughing."

Louis and Keely were not interested in politics. To them, JFK was just another handsome, tomcatting rake from Washington, D.C., having fun in Vegas. Louis, especially, was much more interested in the next gig and what the act would be paid for it than who would be the next president. The Chief probably also thought that he had to be a bigger star than Kennedy—how often had this Massachusetts guy been on Ed Sullivan's show compared to him and Keely?

Because of Sullivan, Prima could keep making triumphant returns to New York. The stone-faced but canny impresario recognized a very simple formula: when Louis and Keely and Sam with the band appeared on his Sunday evening show, ratings went up. As a result, Sullivan tried to book "The Wildest" as often as possible. Sullivan even linked the couple with Elvis Presley, writing in his *New York Daily News* column that those two acts were guaranteed ratings winners for his show.

As good as the national exposure was, Louis was reluctant to accept every invitation from Sullivan because of his fear of flying. In addition, with such a round-trip to New York by train taking up to two weeks, the TV gig by itself didn't come close to paying what the band would earn during the same amount of time in Reno or Chicago or Los Angeles—and, of course, New Orleans—especially with Sullivan being at least as tight-fisted as Louis was.

This *Fabulous Las Vegas* item shows their solution: "Another Casbar Theatre headlining act had a big night last Sunday as Louis Prima and Keely Smith plus Sam Butera and the Witnesses guested on 'smiley' Ed Sullivan's show. Louis and Keely finished first at the Copacabana in New York and made another appearance with Sullivan before returning to FLV and the Sahara." They managed to appear on Sullivan's show eight times, but they could easily have doubled that.

Louis shaved a year off his age by claiming to have been born in 1911, sometimes 1912—and by claiming that he still had a full head of hair, though he had begun wearing a toupee in 1951. The fiction that Keely was born in 1932 still held. In their act, they wrung every ounce out of the aging lothario trying to seduce the sexy, somewhat younger woman scenario. It was a bit too lowbrow for some critics. In "The Wages of Vulgarity" in the September 7, 1959, issue, *Time* magazine sniffed, "The brassy, bulb-nosed, toupeed trumpeter, seeming like a frayed hangover from the night before, began to sing and prance. Somehow, his grinding, gravel-voiced antics made the simple lyrics of 'When You're Smiling' as suggestive as the spiel of a strip-show pitchman. Across the stage, his partner stirred, scratched herself, smothered a belch."

The review also referred, inaccurately, to Louis as a "ham-and-egger for two decades," overlooking his success in the 1940s, and said that after his big band flopped in the '40s (another inaccuracy) he "hammered out garlicky dialogue records of little appeal." Prima's Sahara success was attributed to his being "that rare commodity, an entertainer whose bull bellow can be heard above the rattle and clank of the slot machines."

Stung by the magazine's contempt—though not enough to change the act's winning, if vulgar, formula—the couple turned to the hometown press for relief. "Louis Prima and Keely Smith are hopping mad," began Ken Hansen's column in the *Las Vegas Review-Journal*, "over a highly uncomplimentary article which appeared in a national news magazine. Louis' smile and Keely's poker face turn to deep frowns when they think of *Time* writer Bill Johnson, who the couple says pulled 'quite a twist' on them and turned out to be a 'liar.'" The piece went on to detail their feeling of betrayal because of Johnson's raves to them after seeing their act. "According to Louis, 'Either somebody wrote it for him, or something's wrong with his mind.'"

Even before the *Time* review appeared, Louis and Keely had decided it was time to give up the lounge life. They could make more money and work less by playing a main showroom, and certainly by now they were popular enough that they could draw a big crowd. As the *Time* review indicated, with their contract with the Sahara set to expire, they were being courted by the Sands, the Desert Inn, the Flamingo, and the Sahara.

They conceivably didn't need a base in Las Vegas at all. The act was on the road a lot, performing sold-out shows in the major cities. But Las Vegas anchored them—in addition to having become their home most of the year (when not at the Pretty Acres estate in Louisiana), both of their children had been born there.

Socially, though, it didn't really matter. Keely continued to focus her time and energy on Toni and Luanne when not performing. Louis tended to business. "I don't think he had any friends," Keely once reflected. "He would have golf partners, but I can't think of one real male friend."

Las Vegas was their professional headquarters and a large part of their identity. Along with Sinatra and his group, Louis and Keely had become the public face of a city that rivaled Broadway and Hollywood as epicenters of popular culture in America in the late 1950s.

Prima agreed to a contract from Wilbur Clark to perform at his Desert Inn, in the main showroom. "The Wildest" would do a dinner show at 8:15 and a late show at 11:45, with a 2:15 A.M. show on Fridays. Bill Miller had moved on from the Sahara, but still, it might seem that Louis chose the loot over loyalty. The Sahara, however, wanted Louis and Keely to remain in the lounge and offered that level of money, while Clark offered a five-year, three-million-dollar deal for them as headliners twelve weeks a year with the promise of a three-year extension. Such a deal meant they were set at least until 1967, and for the first five years of the contract they would make fifty thousand a week, with forty weeks a year available to them for shows elsewhere, movies, and recording sessions. Only a handful of performers were being offered not only that amount of money but that length of commitment.

The increased pay would come in handy. The couple's house on Barbara Drive in Las Vegas was beginning to feel confining as Toni and Luanne grew, and Louis had his eye on a piece of land on a golf course.

Plus, Hansen reported, "Keely says she would like to have two more children, and the settling-down effect of more purchases here would fit in with the wish."

With some sadness, Louis and the band bid good-bye to the Sahara after throwing a "jubilee," reminiscent of early Famous Door days, in mid-

September 1959. "The farewell show presented by Louis Prima and Keely Smith, which ended their five-year association with the Sahara, was indeed a gasser," reported the *Review-Journal*. "The popular pair powered their final stand by performing from 2:30 until 5 A.M. in a private party affair. They gave everyone champagne and lavished gifts among hotel employees as they said ta-ta in the place that carried them to stardom and placed the Casbar Theatre in bold letters among the entertainment world's outstanding showcases."

During the show they were joined onstage by Sammy Davis Jr., Dick Shawn, Jerry Colonna (who had helped found the Famous Door in 1935), and Dan Dailey. In the audience that night were Betty Grable, Keely's brother Piggy, and other stars and friends who had become regulars in the lounge. Louis and Keely would be replaced in the Casbar Theatre by the emerging singer and composer Mel Tormé.

The Desert Inn was packed on December 29 when Louis and Keely and Sam and the Witnesses made their debut there. Clark had taken out ads promoting the "gala premiere" that also wished "a happy new year to all!" To all who watched "The Wildest," it looked like it would indeed be one.

No one would have a better year in 1960 than John F. Kennedy. He made numerous quick getaways to Las Vegas to visit with Sinatra and the rest of the Rat Pack. When Kennedy came to town, the group sometimes referred to themselves as the Jack Pack. He enjoyed the showgirls who were only too ready to accommodate a good friend of Frank's. Through Vegas connections, Kennedy began his affair with Judith Campbell, who was also a girlfriend of Sam Giancana's. Sinatra had introduced her to both men.

Kennedy either wasn't aware of how much of Las Vegas was in the mob's pocket—and so too his new pal Sinatra—or refused to think any of it would rub off on him. J. Edgar Hoover, the director of the FBI, kept a huge file on Sinatra that would eventually become the largest on any entertainer in U.S. history.

Kennedy was in the audience on February 8 when the Rat Pack gave one of its shows at the Sands. During 1960, however, while Kennedy continued to enjoy the nightlife with his brother-in-law Lawford as a sort of chaperone, there was a very practical reason for his visits: cash. He wanted to wrest the Democratic nomination for president away from such contenders as Estes

Kefauver and Lyndon Johnson and then campaign against the likely Republican nominee, Richard Nixon. Those efforts would require a lot of money.

Sinatra controlled the cash spigot in Las Vegas, and pretty much anywhere else he went too. He collected that cash as donations and from doing fundraising shows. When Kennedy or a representative was in Vegas, he would literally be handed valises and even shopping bags of cash. Most of the city pulled for Kennedy. A group that included Wilbur Clark raised fifteen million dollars for the Kennedy campaign.

In the days leading up to the election on November 8, 1960, millions of dollars in bets were placed on Kennedy and Nixon, even though it was illegal in Nevada to wager on elections. The night before, the odds were 3–2 in Kennedy's favor. As it turned out, Nevada was the only state in the West that Kennedy won, by fewer than nineteen hundred votes.

26

The main showroom act at the Desert Inn was much more lavish than a small band crowding onto an especially small stage in the Casbar Lounge. Louis had conceived of a production titled "Ship's Log" that included the Donn Arden Dancers and Carlton Hayes and His Orchestra. Keely strutted about in a shorter dress than before to show off her legs. Louis announced on opening night, "I'll have to watch my lingo now—I'm in the big room." Another change was that, because of more space, Louis and Keely often sang apart from each other on two separate microphones. Few knew how truly symbolic this was.

After "The Wildest" opened in December, Louis told Ken Hansen about being in the showroom that "it's not as much of a ball—you don't change as much as you do in the lounge. In the big room, everything you do is planned. In the lounge you might plan something, and some guy gets up and hollers for a scotch and soda during the act, and you have to change the plan for him."

The roster of "The Wildest" underwent changes. Morgan Thomas came aboard on alto saxophone and other wind instruments. John Nagy had replaced Robert Carter on keyboards. Paul Ferrara went back to New Orleans, where he became a twenty-year fixture on drums in Al Hirt's band—in 2009, he and Hirt (posthumously) would be inducted together into the New Orleans Music Hall of Fame—and was replaced by Bobby Morris. (Jimmy Vincent would return to Louis in 1962 for a twelve-year stint.) And on bass was Rolando "Rolly Dee" DiLorio, who would spend fifteen years with Prima and was the only sideman who the Chief treated as something like a friend, or at least more than just a coworker.

Louis and Keely's absence at the Sahara offered an opportunity for Don Rickles, whom *Fabulous Las Vegas* reported was "currently starring in the Casbar Theatre of the Hotel Sahara . . . this time for only a two-week stint." The reviewer urged "all those who have not had the opportunity to catch this comedy wizard's novel act, do so before the master insulter vacates the premises on August 10."

Like many other entertainers, Rickles wanted to be in the Rat Pack's orbit when they were in town. "The Sands was swanky, the hottest spot in town," he recalled. "In those days, the place had strolling violinists and hors d'oeuvres in the lounge."

Another perk was that Sinatra was headlining there, so Rickles took a woman he was infatuated with to the Sands. "We sat in a corner and I ordered champagne. (You can bet it wasn't Dom Perignon.) You could hear the clinking of glasses. You could see this was class."

She was excited to see that Sinatra and his entourage were sitting in a roped-off section. Rickles realized if he could get just a hello from the Chairman of the Board, he would thoroughly impress the woman. He approached Sinatra's table and whispered his request.

Fifteen minutes later, after draining another Jack Daniel's, Sinatra sauntered over to the couple's table. "Don," he said. "How the hell are you?"

Loudly, Rickles responded, "Not now, Frank—can't you see I'm with somebody!"

"The violins stopped. The clinking glasses stopped. Everyone stopped talking. Everyone stared at us. Time stopped. And then, God bless him, Frank fell down laughing."

The Strip was now catering to all tastes, and there were more stages than ever. At the New Frontier the headliner was comedienne and singer Frances Faye. Her backup singing group was the Millionaires, which allowed future comedian Pete Barbutti to make his Las Vegas debut, though it wasn't an auspicious one.

"Frances came in the first day for rehearsal and told us that we had to move to the back of the stage to make room for her grand piano," he recalls. "We couldn't turn up the mikes back there because they were feeding back. So when the show opens, the audience couldn't see us and they could barely hear us. Right away I hated Las Vegas. Finally, I was so aggravated that I went to the front of the stage, grabbed the microphone, and told the audience that this was the stupidest hotel I'd ever been in and the stupidest act I'd ever worked with. It turned out that Bill Miller, who was the entertainment director of the New Frontier then, signed us and got rid of Frances."

At the Riviera, Harry Belafonte reigned. The ageless Marlene Dietrich was at the Sahara. Danny Thomas held court at the Sands. The Silver Slipper had stripper Sally Rand and retired boxer-turned-comic "Slapsy Maxie" Rosenbloom. Pat Brady, the longtime sidekick of Roy Rogers, told jokes and tossed his rope at the Showboat. The 1940s Hollywood actress June Havoc trotted out a show at the Thunderbird. Making men drool at the Tropicana was Jayne Mansfield in a revue titled "French Dressing."

At the Desert Inn were Jimmy Durante and Sonny King. Joe E. Lewis, despite increasing problems with alcohol and diabetes, still managed to perform at El Rancho Vegas. The Ritz Brothers were at the Flamingo. The racy "Minsky Follies" featuring Lou Costello was the main act at the Dunes. Betty Hutton replaced Dietrich at the Sahara, and Red Skelton came in after Belafonte at the Riviera. Prima's hero Louis Armstrong did three weeks at the Sands.

The crowds still packed in to see "The Wildest," but even Louis and Keely headed to the Sands for the Rat Pack performances. In the four weeks that Sinatra and his pals played the hotel during the filming of *Ocean's Eleven*, they drew an audience of thirty-four thousand people.

In a typical scene, Dean Martin wheeled out a table with a full bar on it. He said, "Frank, do you know how to make a fruit cordial?"

"No, Dean. How do you make a fruit cordial?"

Martin paused and shrugged. "Well," he said, "be nice to him."

Another time Martin would flex his arms and ask Sinatra, "You know how I got these muscles?" "No. How, Dean?" "By carrying Jerry all those years."

Sinatra was in the midst of a thirteen-year run as part owner of the hotel. He brought in the high rollers, and thus the mob-controlled consortium that owned the Sands was fine with him being vice-president of the corporation and being paid one hundred thousand dollars a week for performing (and he was given a token of three thousand a night to spend at the gaming tables). The owners had a three-bedroom suite constructed for him with a private swimming pool and health club with a sauna and steam bath. Italian delicacies from New York were flown in especially for him. His performer friends were treated like members of the king's royal court, unless one accepted a gig at another casino. Then Frank beheaded him or her professionally. If Frank liked you, it was anything goes.

"By now, I've been playing the lounge a couple of years," wrote Rickles. "I've built up a little reputation. For the first time, they've even slapped on a cover charge. It's only five bucks, but it makes me feel good. I'm no longer free. You have to buy me. Things are going good."

Until one night when two Nevada state troopers stepped onstage, grabbed the comedian, and walked him out of the Sahara. In a car with the siren blaring, he was driven down the Strip to the Sands, "where I'm taken to Sinatra's table. Frank is sitting with Dean Martin and a trio of gorgeous gals. 'Anything wrong, Don?' asks Sinatra. 'Not at all, Frank. Who needs a job at the Sahara anyway?' Sinatra looks up and smiles. 'I figured as much.'"

Rickles soon ended up with a better job. In addition to his pre–*Tonight Show* TV work, Johnny Carson, who continued to enjoy heckling Rickles in the Casbar Lounge, had become a popular stand-up comedian. One week while he was booked into the Congo Room at the Sahara, he was felled by a sudden illness. The hotel needed a replacement fast, and it reached into the lounge. The Rickles debut in the main showroom was so well received that his days as a lounge act came to an end.

"That day the headliner crapped out and they put Don in the main room," recalls Jack Carter. "The rest is history. He was ready for his big break when it came."

In 1960, the impression among people in America who followed such things was that everyone who was anyone in entertainment played Las Vegas. Televisions had become typical fixtures in American homes, and the variety shows plucked performers from the casinos and put them in front of the cameras every week. Between the two venues, if you were a name in the business it was difficult *not* to make a living.

However, though the money flowed ever faster into entertainers' pockets, not everyone enjoyed performing in Las Vegas. According to Lena Horne, "Las Vegas came to be a symbol of a great deal I hated in this business. It was and is where the big money is for an entertainer. I played the Sands for a decade. It was a beautifully run room, very classy. If you have to play Vegas that is the room to play. But to me there was no gratification to performing there. You never know when you're working in Vegas quite what's happening to you. The audience is a captive one, but the thing that has captured them is the gambling. They really only come to see you in order to take a rest from the crap tables, they aren't thinking about you particularly. There's no challenge in them, so you have no sense of discovery about your performance to gain through their reactions."

Her typical outlook when she was nearing an engagement was, "Oh, it's a waste of time, but I'm going to Vegas." Horne didn't particularly care for Frank Sinatra and his cronies, but she acknowledged that it was largely because of his clout along the Strip that many of the racist restrictions in Las Vegas had fallen by the wayside.

The most eccentric agent of change—though it had nothing to do with racism—in Las Vegas was Howard Robard Hughes. (Coincidentally, he was portrayed by Jason Robards in the 1980 film *Melvin and Howard*.) Hughes's father had created a company in Texas that had as its biggest asset the drill bit, which was purchased in mass quantities by the petroleum industry. At eighteen, his parents dead, he bought out relatives to become the controlling owner of Hughes Tool. He went on to be hugely successful in careers that included engines and weapons manufacturing and movie producing.

One of his screen efforts was *Las Vegas Story*, released in 1952. It is a bland imitation of *Casablanca*, with the Flamingo substituting for Rick's Place. The reason for the film was Jane Russell, Hughes's lady love, who played the Ingrid Bergman role. She had to choose between the Bogie-like Victor Mature and Vincent Price. The only reason to see the movie today is Hoagy Carmichael, who sings and wisecracks his way through the picture.

Hughes had earned a well-deserved reputation as a womanizer; since the 1940s he had been the kid with the big sweet tooth, and Vegas was the candy shop. But by the late '50s, after a 1957 marriage to Jean Peters performed in a Nevada ghost town that, not surprisingly, didn't last, Hughes became more interested in acquiring property than women.

Well, almost. Tony Martin, a longtime favorite of Hughes, tells a story about the making of *Two Tickets to Broadway* in 1957. Even though the singer had taken Cyd Charisse away from Hughes and married her, the two men remained friends. One night while Martin was singing at the Flamingo, Hughes sent for him.

According to Martin, "It was a command appearance. I went. Hughes always used Mormons as his men, because they neither smoked nor drank and he considered them exceptionally trustworthy. He spoke in a soft, high-pitched voice. He had ear trouble and so did I, so we both started aiming our conversation at the other guy's good ear."

Hughes offered the singer seventy-five thousand dollars for the eight-week film shoot. Martin accepted. What he later learned was that Hughes was infatuated with Janet Leigh, who had signed on as the female lead. He planned to shoot the picture indefinitely so that it would come between her and Tony Curtis, they would break up, and Hughes would pounce. It didn't turn out that way, and, against the odds (and Hughes), the picture finally wrapped. "His unrequited crush on Janet Leigh must have cost him millions, but that was the way he was," Martin reported.

But Hughes's heart was really about money and property. "Many times, when I worked in Las Vegas, I'd get a summons from Howard to meet him after my last show," Martin recalled in *The Two of Us*, his memoir with Charisse. "It would be about three in the morning. He'd have his old Chevy there, and I'd sit next to him. We'd drive around for an hour or so. The thing he liked to do best was to show me how much land he owned. 'I own everything from here to the mountains,' he'd say, gesturing with his arm to the mountains which loomed miles away in the moonlight. He wasn't saying it as a braggart would; it was just a statement of simple fact."

Even the mob changed as the new decade began. Shirley MacLaine waxed nostalgic in her *My Lucky Stars* memoir: "When The Boys ran Vegas, they knew how to do it. Their hotels didn't care about a show room paying for itself. Gambling and a good time were the high priorities. The showroom and its entertainers were there to get you in the mood to drop your cash on the green velvet tables. If you were stupid enough to fall for it, that was their gain. Vegas was one of the only towns in the world that told the truth about itself. . . . Everything was designed to make you have such a good time you'd even enjoy your losses, and furthermore you were warned."

A new generation of entertainers, still wet behind the ears, arrived in town looking to make an impression, sometimes finding that Las Vegas didn't impress them. "I was disappointed in Las Vegas," recalled Wayne Newton in *Once Before I Go*, who with his brother, Jerry, opened their act at the Fremont two weeks after he quit high school in his junior year in 1959. "I thought the Dunes Hotel should have been big sandhills with a door. I thought the Flamingo should have been a big bird with the elevator going up the leg. At least the Showboat should have been a real showboat in the water."

Demonstrating how things had expanded since the Mary Kaye Trio and "The Wildest," the Newton Brothers were just one of four lounge acts at the Fremont, the others being Glenn Smith and the Fables, the Jets, and the Makebelievers. It could be a tough place for a sixteen-year-old kid.

"The stage was set on a high platform, with the bartender standing below us mixing drinks, and the audience sat looking up at us," according to Newton. "Some women would sit there at the bar and open up the tops of their dresses. We were the only ones who could see it. I was propositioned a lot, but I was too naïve to know it. It never occurred to me that any of the flirting was being directed at me.

"When I wasn't looking down the front of ladies' dresses, I was trying to finish high school by correspondence during the first year or two, an effort that didn't prove too successful." The good news was the act earned $280 a week in what ultimately was a forty-six-week booking, pretty good for a couple of teenagers from Phoenix in 1959 and '60.

While Las Vegas had been no secret to much of America during the 1950s, it would be truly discovered by everyone in the '60s and beyond thanks to television and an expanding entertainment media, leading to the overdeveloped, water-parched mini-metropolis it is today. In 1960, when Louis Prima and Keely Smith and the Witnesses were at the height of their fame, the population of the Las Vegas metropolitan area was 127,016, up from 5,165 thirty years earlier; by 1995, the population had hit the million mark.

Was "The Wildest" among the changes affecting Las Vegas? No. One would think that after six years they would make significant changes in their repertoire to keep audiences coming back. True, they made tweaks because of the move to the Desert Inn. And there was still improvisation within each show, though the players performed the script as written by Prima. There was no need to change, because what "The Wildest" delivered was what visitors from around the country wanted. Even after six years, the act had yet to get old. Prima's North Star had always been to perform with an uncanny freshness what people wanted to hear and see.

"The whole thing kept working," says Jack Carter. "You knew what you were going to get and still you couldn't wait to see it. You knew that Keely was going to stand there and stare at him, and Louis was going to do dumb things and ad-lib. And he always tried to be dirty—'Ba-bum, up your ass' and 'Kiss my ass.' He'd try to break her up and the band was great. That is what the audience came for night after night after night."

The act stayed the same and kept working also because Keely could play her part flawlessly night after night, and both men and women in the audience loved the character she portrayed. "Keely played the role assigned to her extremely well," says Bruce Raeburn. "She was attractive, sexy, and exercised extreme self-control as a poker face while continually under comedic assault by Prima. Imagine withstanding that mugging without cracking up. Meanwhile, she also came across as almost virginal in contrast to his very libidinous antics. She was an accomplished actress as well as a good vocalist, playing cool and aloof to Prima's hot and agitated flawlessly."

However, there were about to be many changes offstage.

27

Louis had attempted sailing again in the summer of 1959. In what could have been seen as a bad omen about his and Keely's marriage, the results were similar to his failed voyage with Tracelene thirteen years earlier. This time, with Keely, Louis took a $160,000 yacht down the Atlantic coastline and once more grounded the boat. They sat on it, embarrassed, until the coast guard came to their rescue.

There exists a strange photo of the couple taken in May 1960 that hinted all was not well. Louis is standing on the right in a white suit holding his trumpet in his left hand; his mouth is wide open, and he is leering at Keely, standing to his right. She is quite tan and wearing a low-cut white dress. Her expression is disturbing—she is staring straight ahead with what was probably supposed to be passivity or dismissal, but instead she looks genuinely frightened.

Keely maintained to Prima biographer Garry Boulard and others that her husband abruptly began to go out after the Desert Inn shows and spend a lot more time away from their home. Such activities—and she could only guess at half of them—put an increasing strain on the marriage.

"Then all of a sudden—I don't know, it wasn't like an overnight thing, I'm sure it wasn't, but that's how it appeared to me—he started drinking," Keely said. "He started smoking. He started gambling. And he started running all over town with different women. Maybe it was a phase he was going through. I didn't know. But it lasted too long, there was just so much going on, that I wound up sick over it. I tried to talk to him about it and I really don't think that he wanted to do it. I think it was something, he couldn't help himself."

"Whatever happened," said Joe Segreto in *Louis Prima: The Wildest!*, "it began to affect their life together. He and Keely began to unravel."

There are several accounts of Prima stepping out on Keely. He had never been much of a drinker, but that did change. There were innuendos in the local press about Louis sampling the nightlife at several casinos. Louis himself refused to speak to reporters. This had been a longstanding policy of his, not to grant interviews and, with the exception of the *Life* magazine profile in 1956 when the exposure was most beneficial, not to invite profiles of his wife and children.

"When you think about it," muses Mike Weatherford of the *Review-Journal* about Louis's policy, "if he has the 'wildest' show in Las Vegas, it wouldn't help to keep emphasizing that he was a stay-at-home family man."

Control freak that Louis was, part of his policy was that if he did do an interview, he had to approve the piece before publication. Even in Las Vegas, very few editors would agree. Louis kept on feeding PR tidbits to the press, but that was different because it was solely his message and the columnists were always hungry for material. As a result, there does not exist a tell-all or mea culpa article about the problems in the Primas' marriage as would be commonplace today in the media world of Angelina Jolie and Tiger Woods.

Some incidents couldn't be covered up, however. According to one newspaper account on October 7, 1959, "Singers Louis Prima and Keely Smith were sued in district court today by a collection agent for $1131.39 for clothing sold to the couple earlier this year. The claim states that Miss Smith purchased goods between Apr. 9 and July 6 at Sydney's Proginals, Inc., costing $1106.71, and that Prima purchased an item for $24.68 on Jan. 26. Also asked for is $350 in fee for Atty. John Sullivan, who prepared the action." In February 1960, the court found for the plaintiff. Presumably the couple paid the bill.

Whatever her own misbehavior—she has always been close-mouthed about her contributions to the friction between them—Keely blamed Louis for all their problems. She contended many years later, "He was being . . . not nice. He expected things. He didn't like to pay bills. It was the case of the star starting to believe that the world revolves around him."

"I was hearing from the guys that it was bad," said drummer Paul Ferrara, who heard the gossip back in Al Hirt's band in New Orleans. "I'm hearing that Louis started screwing around more. I think Louis at that time was still so hungry to make it—like, nothing was ever going to be enough—and so self-obsessed with it, that he started to let his self-discipline go, little by little. For Keely, what did she know about handling this?"

There were more whispers about an affair that she was supposedly having with Sinatra, and Keely did nothing to dispel them.

The Primas' marital problems earning attention along the Strip raise the question of whether their love story was always a sham, another showbiz prop to make an act seem better.

Everything Keely said and did from the time she met Louis through the 1950s testifies to her genuinely being in love with him. She would learn that at times it had been an obsessive, unhealthy love that cost her some of herself. Years later, she said in an interview about her husband, "He had me so brainwashed over who I was. I believed everything he said." Still, her declarations of love sounded sincere.

It could have been a different story with Louis. Undoubtedly, he was attracted to Keely's talent. The way audiences related to her meant, first, that when they were a twosome he could keep his career going when it was otherwise draining away, and, second, that his second (or third) act as a performer could be an even bigger success. For someone so obsessed with his career and his popularity, Louis had to appreciate and probably love what Keely brought to their union.

The sexual attraction between them was not faked in the act, so that was an important part of the relationship. Probably Louis, as was his pattern, wanted more variety, and because Keely was beautiful and special in many respects, it took him quite a bit longer to revert to his tomcat ways. So what about love? Maybe Prima showed how he felt the best way he knew—by singing and dancing with his wife night after night and playing pretty for the people.

It was business as usual onstage for "The Wildest" as the couple dismissed the occasional query from the press about their marriage. During an appearance on *The Ed Sullivan Show* that fall of 1960, Louis and Keely's performance was so well received that the audience, messing with the host's schedule, demanded an encore. They came back out onstage and sang "I'm Confessin' That I Love You."

Back in Las Vegas, produced by what was now called Keelou Productions, was another extravaganza ready for the Desert Inn in December 1960. The new act conceived by Louis was "The Frantic Forties."

This wouldn't seem like much of a stretch, considering that Prima had played a significant role in the entertainment of the 1940s, but that was fine with him. He was giving the audiences what they wanted by playing the nostalgia card. Back came the Donn Arden Dancers and Carlton Hayes and His Orchestra, who had been part of the first Desert Inn production. The new year, with a friend and Las Vegas fan installed as president, looked very promising—professionally, at least.

28

The year 1961 was going to be an especially important one for the world as well as for Louis and Keely. Adolf Eichmann would be tried in Jerusalem for war crimes. Yuri Gagarin would become the first human to orbit the earth, and a month later, in May, Alan Shepard would become the first American to do it. There would be the disastrous Bay of Pigs invasion. Gary Cooper would die, as would Ty Cobb, who was a member of the first class of Baseball Hall of Famers in 1933. Pope John XXIII would issue a ban on birth control a year after the pill was approved by the U.S. Food and Drug Administration. And both the United States and the Soviet Union would renew nuclear testing (bringing mushroom clouds back to Nevada), coinciding with a series of confrontations in Berlin.

And it all began with the inauguration of a new president. For his pal Jack Kennedy, the party that night at the Washington Armory was going to be the biggest one that Frank ever threw. Sinatra wanted only the best in everything, especially the performers, and of course he wanted Louis Prima and Keely Smith to be there. And of course they would say yes and leave Las Vegas on the train and bring their act east. Sinatra wanted public credit for his devotion and loyalty to the cause of ushering in a new and hip administration. The payback was arranged: Frank would produce a show for the inauguration like nothing Washington, D.C., had ever seen before, and the president would attend as the guest of honor.

Old Blue Eyes did his part. He cajoled and persuaded and called in markers, and in a few cases he ordered A-list entertainers to be there or else they wouldn't be as welcome in Las Vegas or Hollywood as before. Ella Fitzgerald flew in from Australia, Shirley MacLaine from Japan, Gene Kelly from Switzerland, Sidney Poitier from France, and predictably there was a large contingent from Las Vegas, ready to remind the Kennedys how cash had flowed into the campaign's coffers throughout 1960.

Louis, sometimes with Keely, had participated in Democratic fundraisers during the 1960 campaign. He wasn't necessarily political, but JFK was certainly more favored in Las Vegas entertainment circles than Richard Nixon, and, more important, Sinatra was his biggest backer. Being closer to the Chairman of the Board, Louis knew, could only be good for business—the hell with the rumors about his wife and Sinatra.

The night of January 20, 1961, there was a furious snowstorm in Washington, D.C., but the show went ahead anyway. Among those in attendance from Las Vegas was Howard Hughes, who sat in one of the four inaugural boxes that his company had bought for ten thousand dollars each.

The time came when Joey Bishop introduced Louis and Keely, promising that Sam Butera and the Witnesses "won't take the Fifth." Their performance had people wearing tuxedos and gowns dancing in the aisles. Afterward, Sinatra presented Louis and Keely along with other performers a silver cigarette box. If the event had included a visit to the White House, of the performers only Prima would have had the distinction of being the guest of both FDR (in 1944) and JFK.

But everything was about to change between Sinatra and the Kennedys. The first problem was the mixture of black and white skin. Many reports over the years have maintained that Sammy Davis Jr. did not attend the inaugural gala because Washington (not to mention Southern politicians and their constituents) was still not ready for black and white performers sharing the same stage even though people like Lena Horne, Ella Fitzgerald, Nat King Cole, and others had appeared on television shows hosted by white performers. As recently as 1958, when Perry Como accidentally touched Horne's arm while performing a song on his TV show, the network was flooded with angry letters and telegrams.

However, during the gala Harry Belafonte, Sidney Poitier, and Ella Fitzgerald were among the African Americans who took to the stage. The fact is that Davis was exiled because during the year of the election he had married May Britt, a white actress. Peter Lawford was given the unpleasant task of calling Davis and essentially overriding, on behalf of his brother-in-law the president, Sinatra's invitation to Davis to perform.

Even with Davis's absence and despite Sinatra's helplessness, the gala and the dinner at the Hilton where the new president came to greet Sinatra's guests comprised the peak moment of glory for the singer in his relationship with the Kennedys.

Then it collapsed. The end of the relationship began as soon as a few hours after the dinner ended. Somebody said something to Sinatra, perhaps that he had been disinvited to fly to Palm Beach in the morning with other celebrities to visit with Joseph Kennedy at the patriarch's estate. When the time came to leave, he and Juliet Prowse, his steady girlfriend at the time, stayed in their suite, and Sinatra told those departing that he had to return to Los Angeles.

The rift became wider when Kennedy appointed his brother Bobby as attorney general. Bobby announced that one of his targets would be organized crime, and that inevitably meant going after Sam Giancana. The short-fused mob kingpin believed that he had been double-crossed. Sinatra knew that any further friendliness with the Kennedy clan would be a death sentence. The Hoboken-born Sinatra was not going to be allowed in Camelot. It was one thing for JFK to party off the radar screen in Las Vegas with associates of organized crime, but it was another to be president and have high-profile friends with mob connections.

According to Tony Curtis, "Frank's relationship with Sam Giancana was the reason that Jack Kennedy had been forced to cut Frank off as a friend after he got elected president. J. Edgar Hoover knew all about Frank's mob friends, so he told Kennedy to keep Frank at arm's length, which Kennedy did. That was very hurtful to Frank, who had been an important campaigner for Kennedy, and Frank never forgave Jack for turning his back on him."

Curtis wrote that "Frank took his anger out on Peter Lawford. Once Jack Kennedy severed his ties to Frank, Frank turned right around and cut Peter Lawford out of his life completely. It was as if Peter no longer existed."

Though Sinatra, Martin, and Davis would continue to perform together on stages and TV shows for another thirty-plus years, the popularity of the Rat Pack began to wane as their arrogance increased and their showmanship declined, and that signaled another change in Las Vegas. In May 1961, Eddie Fisher, being paid twenty-five thousand a week, had an engagement at the Desert Inn that was a big comeback for him. His marriage to Elizabeth Taylor and her personal and professional demands had damaged his career. Not knowing that he was soon to be replaced by Richard Burton during the filming of *Cleopatra*, Fisher returned to Vegas to revive that career.

The successful Desert Inn engagement—sandwiched in between runs of "The Wildest" there—led to a series of shows at the Cocoanut Grove in Los Angeles. It was his first appearance there in seven years, when Debbie Reynolds had been his date. This time, Taylor was. Among the famous faces in the audience were John Wayne, Henry Fonda, Kirk Douglas, Groucho Marx, and Yul Brynner. Also, Frank Sinatra was there "with the entire Rat Pack. Now they make movies about them and write books about them, but we had to live with them. There were people who wrote that my opening night at the Cocoanut Grove was the beginning of the end of the Rat Pack," according to Fisher.

"They started heckling me the moment I walked out on stage. They were all drunk. When I started singing 'That Face' to Elizabeth, Dean yelled out, 'If I were you, I wouldn't be working. I'd be home with her.' That's the clean version that was reported. And Dean was my friend. Eventually they took over the stage."

Feeling helpless to stem the Rat Pack tide, Fisher took a seat and became a member of the audience. Sinatra and his pals, fueled by alcohol and ego, let themselves go, with the result being a torrent of racial and ethnic insults, vulgar limericks, imitations of some of the celebs in the audience, and slurring their way through several songs. "At times they had been clever and funny, but most of the people in this audience had seen their act many times before," Fisher wrote. "These celebrities had come to see Eddie Fisher sing love songs to Elizabeth Taylor, not a drunken fraternity party, and they started booing them."

The Rat Pack had one more big event in them. Sinatra and company were filming a movie in Utah that would be released as *Sergeants 3*. Because of the distance, they would not show up at the Sands every night as they did during the shooting of *Ocean's Eleven*. But the hotel let word get around that something special could happen there on June 7, which was Dean Martin's forty-fourth birthday. On that night over two thousand people tried to squeeze into the Sands showroom, and most had to be turned away. Among those who made it in were Marilyn Monroe and, apparently not holding a grudge after the Cocoanut Grove experience, Eddie Fisher and Elizabeth Taylor.

Sure enough, Sinatra emerged and sang and smoked his way through a dozen songs. Martin was there too, and, called to the stage to serenade him, using lyrics written by Sammy Cahn, were Fisher, Lawford, Bishop, and Vic Damone. A birthday cake resembling a bottle of J&B Scotch that was five feet tall was brought out. Martin threw a slice at Sammy Davis Jr., who threw it back, and a food fight broke out.

The fighting between Louis and Keely involved more than food, and it quickly intensified. It became harder for Keely to be onstage with her husband, and she suffered frequent bouts of stress-related illness. In March, Louis and Sam and the Witnesses traveled to Miami, where a lucrative gig at the Fontainebleau Hotel awaited them. Keely, instead of joining them, went to Los Angeles. Louis began the engagement without her. Inevitably there came questions from the press.

At first he told the *New York Post* that he had been booked at the hotel as a single act and Keely was not involved. He claimed that Dean Martin was supposed to do the engagement, but when he had to drop out for another commitment, Louis filled in. Next, Louis told reporters that Keely had a staph infection and was being treated by a Los Angeles specialist. "We're in harmony," he insisted.

But innuendos about them splitting up persisted, so Keely flew to Miami and finished the gig with Louis. One night, while she was onstage, Louis stopped the show to shout at a columnist in the audience who had printed the word *divorce* that it was "ridiculous" to print such lies. He vowed that they would return to the Desert Inn—and the three-million-dollar contract—"as Mr. and Mrs. Prima."

They did, but that Louis and Keely were barely still together was a common topic of conversation in Las Vegas. When not onstage, Keely continued to keep to herself and her daughters. This was not unusual, but she now had even more reason not to be exposed to the public. She began to think that she wanted out of a marriage that was suddenly in freefall before her health was shot entirely.

"I told him I could not handle any of this," she revealed to Garry Boulard in a 1986 interview. "And I said I wanted a divorce. He wanted a divorce too, but then he turned around and said he wanted to stay together. I was so hurt and my stomach was in knots and I just didn't want to be involved with it anymore."

But Keely did stick with it. One reason had to be her daughters, but another was that ever since Louis had hired her in Virginia Beach in 1948, she had been his personally and professionally—and content to be so for most of that time. Now, with the solo albums and TV appearances, her star shone as brightly as her husband's, but it was beyond her imagination to know what to do with herself in her own solar system. As she had said like a mantra in the few interviews she had done over the years, "I'm nothing without Louis Prima." Thus they continued their frolicking at the Desert Inn and at clubs around the country.

Louis did not make a similar effort to keep the marriage going. No longer a homebody when offstage, he was seen drinking at other casinos and at parties accompanied by women. Years later, in interviews Keely contended that her husband at fifty exhibited signs of "male menopause." This might seem trite, and it was unheard-of in the 1960s, but it did seem to be the case that Prima, after knowing Keely for thirteen years and being married to her for eight, was feeling anxiety about getting older. The aging lothario he had played onstage for all those years he now played offstage, seeking approval not from his wife but from young women who were starstruck when he bought them drinks after the show.

They were due back again at the Fontainebleau Hotel. Keely was too heartsick to go. Yet an intact "Wildest" did perform there.

"I've never told this one before," says Debbie Reynolds. "They were booked for a week at the Fontainebleau in Miami, and Keely got sick. I knew the act so well that Louis called me in California and begged me to fly east and do Keely's part. I only found out later that she and Louis were so on the ropes by then that she wasn't sick, she just couldn't go on with him. So I did a week being Keely Smith—I wore a black wig and her full poodle skirt and my impression of her, and for the five days the audience didn't know that it was Debbie Reynolds and not Keely Smith. It went so well that Louis asked me to stay, but I had film commitments and young children at home, and I just couldn't do it. But I had a great time. And because no one knew I wasn't Keely, Louis got paid."

To this day, Reynolds says, "I doubt that Keely ever knew that I did it. I'm sorry that they ever broke up. I loved them both. And they had the greatest act."

In August 1961, news broke that the Primas' golf course house, which was not yet completed, was up for sale, fueling more reports like one in the *Las Vegas Review-Journal* that "entertainers Louis Prima and Keely Smith will break up professionally." Grimly, the couple prepared for their next stint at the Desert Inn that month.

When that gig ended in September, so did the marriage. Louis rented an apartment off the Strip and moved into it on October 1. Just two days later, either as a kneejerk reaction or a long-planned move, Keely filed for divorce.

The story of the divorce ran in the *New York Times* and other major newspapers around the country and appeared on the front pages of the Las Vegas newspapers. At the very least, what took place inside a courtroom on October 3 demonstrated how liberal the Nevada divorce laws really were: Keely filed the suit in the morning, and Judge Taylor Wines granted the decree that same afternoon. She had charged "extreme cruelty, entirely mental in character . . . causing great unhappiness and injury to plaintiff's health." She claimed that Louis stayed out all night and neglected her and Toni and Luanne.

Keely wore a puffed-out light-colored dress with a checkered pattern and white shoes, and clutched a white purse as she left the courthouse. Especially noticeable were the large, dark sunglasses that hid her red eyes. Walking past reporters, she managed to choke out, "I never actually thought it would happen . . . but I guess it's best for all of us."

She told reporters that she would continue to live in the still-unfinished house on the Desert Inn golf course with their two daughters. "Everything was very friendly and fair," she said about the fifteen-minute divorce proceeding, which Louis did not attend. "I think I'm going to do a TV show," Keely said about her immediate plans as a performer. When asked if she would ever share a stage with Louis again, she replied, "Gee, I don't know."

It was an abrupt end to the real "Wildest," though the name would live on. "Prima and Miss Smith were riding the crest of popularity for their act at the Desert Inn, which included Sam Butera and the Witnesses," reported the *Review-Journal*. "They closed an eight-week engagement at the hotel Monday night, and Prima is slated to appear later this month at a Los Angeles nitery with Butera and his musical group." So even though the headline in the *Las Vegas Sun* read "Keely Smith Sheds Prima," Louis and the band both were leaving her behind too.

Two days later Keely arrived in Los Angeles, appearing to be in the midst of a breakdown. She got off the plane clearly exhausted and weeping and was embraced by Barbara Belle. She was admitted to Cedars of Lebanon Hospital with the excuse again being "minor surgery." She was ill for weeks.

"I felt that Louis was more broken up about what happened, but then again I saw him more than I did Keely after the divorce," says Reynolds. "But I never asked because I didn't feel it was my business."

The year got tougher for Louis when his father, Anthony Prima, passed away at age seventy-four.

In the year-end issue of *Fabulous Las Vegas*, among the ads offering season's greetings was a very simple full-page one. A strip at the top read "Happy Holidays." The rest of the page was a black-and-white illustration of a pageboy haircut, forehead, and dark eyebrows and eyes. The rest of the page was white except for only "Keely" in script.

The portrait was clever and eye-catching, but the partial image could also lead one to wonder if she was fading away.

29

And, much too suddenly, the love story of Louis and Keely was over.

If Louis felt broken up about the divorce, he didn't show it. He forged ahead with plans to continue the act and treated Keely's loss like an annoying distraction that he wished reporters would stop asking him about.

"As their career unwound and they divorced as a married couple, there came some difficult times—much more difficult for Keely at that time than it was for Louis," according to Joe Segreto, who was recruited from New Orleans to become Louis's manager (because by offering Keely a sympathetic shoulder in Los Angeles, Belle, in Prima's eyes, had sided with his ex-wife). "Louis, that cat's got nine lives."

Indeed, printed on new stationary that Prima ordered was "This Cat's Got Nine Lives."

"Louis went through a couple of girls trying to find the one to fill that spot, and he worked for a time with another girl singer," said Segreto in *Louis Prima: The Wildest!* "He still had Sam Butera and the Witnesses. He still had marvelous music to draw on. He still had his own talents. There were some things different, of course. The fans were used to Louis and Keely."

"It was disappointing to us fans when they broke up," says Lorraine Hunt-Bono. "It was very much like when Dean Martin and Jerry Lewis split. It sure felt different on the Strip to not have Louis and Keely performing together."

That difference first became apparent to a national audience when in 1961 the film *Twist All Night* was released, with Prima as the lead. Butera and the Witnesses were again on hand, but this cheesy attempt to ride the coattails of the dance craze created by Chubby Checker's hit single completely lacked the charm and sweetness found in *Hey Boy! Hey Girl!* Any discomfort felt about Louis being the "boy" of the 1959 film's title was exacerbated in the new film as the fifty-year-old awkwardly gyrated with young women, some less than half his age. For those who saw *Twist All Night*, clearly a big piece was missing. It did Prima a favor that not too many people saw it.

Louis's attitude that he was the star and everyone around him mere supporting players was shaken when the Desert Inn cancelled his contract. Wilbur Clark did not want "The Wildest" without Keely, certainly not in the main showroom and for fifty thousand a week. In a rather cruel gesture, the casino's next paycheck to Louis had the figure "$000,000.00" on it. Also cancelled was work on a TV series that had been proposed to Louis and Keely. Club owners around the country who had appreciated what Keely brought to the act removed bookings of "The Wildest" from their schedule. The Dot Records deal was up in the air. Their personal split was professionally going to cost the couple millions of dollars.

Prima's career was far from over, however. He found that he was still somewhat popular as a solo act. Being surrounded onstage by the loyal Butera and the Witnesses helped. Or did it? It was probably impossible for Prima emotionally and financially, but at the time he might have been better off striking out on his own with a new band and reinventing his career once more. Like the movie audience, the stage audience saw the same tried-and-true act, but Keely was missing. He even had to endure hecklers, who asked where Keely was and said "The Wildest" was not as wild without her.

"After the divorce, Louis, when he was away from his Las Vegas power base, seemed like one of the walking dead," wrote Garry Boulard, adding, "Even Prima's continued presence in Las Vegas was suspect. Where once Vegas was portrayed as the home of the hip, to many 1960s kids the gambling mecca was viewed instead as a graveyard of misplaced values, unrealized dreams, and middle-aged juveniles."

With no singers working out, and with Louis offering reporters ridiculous statements about Keely like "We are better off without her," he had to

find a true replacement, and pronto. In 1962, he told reporters he was looking for a new singer. As the items appeared in the press, women sent him
photos and tapes. As he and Sam worked smaller clubs around the country,
he held auditions. The woman he chose, like Keely, was already a big fan of
his, much younger, and very impressionable.

Gia Maione was a waitress whose father was a longtime fan of Prima's.
When she was fourteen, on a family vacation in Florida, her father arranged
an introduction, and Prima signed a photo of himself for her. From that
moment on, Gia recalled in a 2008 interview, "I collected every single recording he ever made. In school, for the variety shows, I would always perform
Louis's music."

Gia saw herself as a singer, having studied voice as well as piano. She was
twenty when she showed up at the door of the Latin Casino in Camden,
where Prima and the band were playing that night. He listened to her sing
and invited her to a lunch show that Mother's Day Sunday at the local B'nai
B'rith. (The venue was surely a sign of how his popularity was waning.)

"I was working as a waitress at Howard Johnson's restaurant at the time,"
Maione recalled. "He called me up during the show, and I think because I
was so young, and naïve, and innocent-looking with the full crinoline skirts,
and the poodle haircut, he thought he was just going to get a kick calling
me up onstage. During the show he asked me if I knew 'I'm in the Mood
for Love,' and I said yes. So he started the intro for it, and of course, I knew
every arrangement, I knew everything, so I just did it. And he would look
at me and then he would look at Sam. Then he said, well, do you know this
song, and I said yes, and so we did the next song. Then he kept me up there
and he went into 'Just a Gigolo' and 'I Ain't Got Nobody,' and I did all of the
backgrounds with the boys. I just knew exactly what to do."

Prima ended up picking her over two other candidates, Michelle Lee and
Charlotte Duber. "He never really told me I got the job," said Gia. "But he
said to my mom and me, 'We're opening at Basin Street East tomorrow. Can
you be here in the parking lot tomorrow morning to take the bus there?' And
of course, I did. It was a Cinderella story come true. And the engagement,
later that week, was *The Ed Sullivan Show*. So that was my first TV show.
My first professional engagement and it was wonderful. Everyone else was a
nervous wreck. I was not."

Gia did have a winning voice and personality, and some critics overlooked Keely's absence. "Louis Prima's excellent new vocalist, pretty Gia Maione of Toms River, N.J., won a standing ovation at her Basin St. East premiere," the *New York Post* reported in its May 15, 1962, edition. "It's a Cinderella tale. The auburn-haired 21-year-old [Prima may have had to add a year to her age] was a hostess in a Howard Johnson restaurant and sang professionally only a few times. She joined Prima four days ago, didn't buy a gown or shoes for last night's opening till 3 P.M. yesterday."

Though young and inexperienced, it appears that Gia was not intimidated following in Keely's footsteps and performing with a band that Keely had fronted for seven years. "I was an entirely different person with an entirely different style of singing," she told Bruce Sylvester in 2003. "The intention was never to duplicate their act. She had a deep, smoky sound. She was a torch singer, but Louis immediately saw that my niche was novelties like 'I Want You to Be My Baby' and 'Goody Goody.' When I was hired, neither Louis nor any of the Witnesses made me feel like I would have to fill her shoes. They immediately respected my style and the way I was, and they helped me mature and grow up as a performer with Louis."

During the next few months, Gia underwent a transformation orchestrated by Prima. There was an odd similarity to what the James Stewart character did to the Kim Novak character in Alfred Hitchcock's 1958 film *Vertigo* in an attempt to resurrect his former lover. Gia's hair got shorter, as did the dresses. The way she was billed on concert posters and TV shows gave her status it took Keely years to earn. Louis was making a statement that Keely had been just one in a line of female singers who had succeeded only because they were in an act with him.

That had been true with the others but not with Keely. Louis had conveniently forgotten where his career was going in 1948, which was musical Palookaville. Keely Smith opened the door that allowed Prima to have that Scott Fitzgerald second act. Gia, as engaging as she was and with a pleasing voice, was not about to give Louis's career a similar boost. This was not her fault—she was genuinely talented—but Prima's career was about to be rocked by a changing cultural landscape.

Soon Prima was acting out another Hollywood film parallel—to *Citizen Kane*. The much older John Foster Kane (Louis was fifty-one to Gia's twenty when they met) is obsessed with establishing his girlfriend as an opera singer, and the results of his hubris are disastrous. While not disastrous, Prima's efforts to create a solo career for Gia were at the very least disappointing. He built a recording studio in the home they were now sharing in Las Vegas and began his own label, Prima One Magnagroove Records, because "the music we're going to put out on this record label is in a large groove." He took six months and employed forty-eight musicians to record Gia's debut as a solo artist, *This Is . . . Gia*. It garnered some good reviews, but consumers didn't take to it.

What did mirror the Louis-Keely dynamic is that Prima fell in love with his singer, and vice versa. "I don't know where idolatry ended and love began," Gia recalled. "We were in Lake Tahoe and it was in between the second and third show and he said, 'Meet me at the side entrance of Harrah's right after this show. Change your clothes and meet me.' So I did."

In February 1963, in a limo being driven to Reno, he proposed. She accepted. They found a justice of the peace in Reno and got married. They returned to Harrah's, and, instead of introducing her as Gia Maione, he said, "Ladies and gentlemen, here's Mrs. Prima."

Before long, Gia made fewer stage appearances, because in the next two years she gave birth to two children, Lena Ann and Louis Jr., Louis's first and only son. Prima was fifty-four when the boy, his sixth and last child, was born in June 1965.

Prima, like many performers whose careers had begun twenty or more years earlier, was nearly crushed by the cultural tsunami that was the Beatles. American radios first began to blare "She Loves You" in the fall of 1963, but the impact was minimal until the following February, when the Fab Four stepped off a jet at John F. Kennedy International Airport in New York and appeared on *The Ed Sullivan Show*, the same program that had kept Prima and his generation of performers in the American entertainment spotlight for a decade. The moment the Pan Am plane from London touched down, everything changed. Prima's act appeared dated, and his attempts to avoid becoming obsolete by changes in toupees and clothing only emphasized that he was thirty years older than John, Paul, George, and Ringo and the British invaders who followed up on the beachhead they established.

"I don't think there was a period when Prima's fortunes really lagged because of the absence of Keely," contended the writer Will Friedwald in the Prima documentary. "Obviously, it was star power, because Keely had been a headliner at that point. The problem with Prima's later career was the onset of this whole other kind of music. There was really not much he could do against the British invasion. There wasn't very much he could do to stay in the limelight at that point and it was the same thing that happened to Frank Sinatra, Tony Bennett, to all the great stars of that period, finding a way to deal with that." The way Prima dealt with that was by concentrating on his core audience in Las Vegas and New Orleans.

Even though the Beatles played a show there, Las Vegas remained a refuge or last outpost of what was becoming a conquered race of entertainers. Acts like Louis Armstrong (before being reclaimed by jazz purists), Nat King Cole, and the Mary Kaye Trio were, in the mid-'60s, the Joe E. Lewis and Sophie Tucker, Ray Bolger, and Jimmy Durante of a decade before in Las Vegas. Would Prima have been more of a survivor if he and Keely had remained together? One has to believe so. She was still in her thirties for most of the 1960s. She most likely would have further established her solo career while also packing the rooms with Louis and Sam.

In the fall of 1965, Prima signed a contract to perform at the Sands Hotel. Sinatra was on hand to mark the occasion, but in a photo taken for publicity purposes his expression is remarkably different than when he appeared in photos with Keely. It's obvious that this was not the way Frank wanted things to turn out.

In connection with the Sands deal, Prima's official biography for the press was revised. It is a breezy and of course effusive overview of his career—among its offerings are, "Along with space travel, the most talked-about subject today is Louis Prima" and he "is easily the youngest living legend in show business"—and concludes with his ongoing collaboration with Gia Maione and Sam Butera. Not anywhere in the three full pages of copy is there a mention of Keely Smith. It read as if he had headlined alone during the 1950s.

Before 1965 was over, Louis's mother, Angelina, died. Louis was devastated and could not bring himself to look at his mother during the wake. He may have felt guilty, too, because Angelina was unhappy when her son and Keely divorced.

Even the welcome mat in Las Vegas began to shrink. But Prima could always go home to New Orleans and find an enthusiastic audience, and he was accompanied by the ever-loyal Sam Butera, though the cast of the Witnesses kept changing.

"We made some arrangements for him to come back to New Orleans, and he would perform most of the year there," said Joe Segreto. "It was a big departure for Louis to want to do that."

But there was one more life to this cat. In 1966, Prima received an invitation from the Walt Disney studio for him and his band to perform for the studio's team of animators. They did, and the result was the creation of the King Louie character that would play an important role in Disney's next animated film, *The Jungle Book*.

Before the movie came out, Prima attempted to create a second life for his animated alter ego. He commissioned a screenplay titled *King Louie the Most*, written by Stephen Lord, in anticipation of capitalizing on the Disney film. It would star Louis and Gia with Sam and the Witnesses. The opening scene has a narrator identified as Louis Armstrong who introduces the audience to the king of Groovesville (Prima) and his royal court: Sampson the Sender, Sir Winston Smirchpill, Sir Walter Rolly, Morgan the Merrier, and Sir Dancelot. In the painful dialogue, Prima tries to come off as a cool '60s swinger.

The Jungle Book was released in November 1967, and Prima had his best big-screen role ever, as a cartoon ape. His rocking rendition of "I Want to Be Like You" is a highlight of the picture. He and costar Phil Harris (the film also featured Sebastian Cabot, George Sanders, and Sterling Holloway) made two successful albums together, and they earned a gold record.

According to a review in the December 11, 1967, issue of *Newsweek* magazine, "At worst, 'The Jungle Book' is an unpretentious and agreeably old-fashioned cartoon. What it lacks in inspiration it mostly makes up for in expertise." And "Louis Prima talks a great game as king of the apes." The *New York Times* was more enthusiastic, calling it a "perfectly dandy cartoon feature" and "grand fun for all ages," as were audiences, who made *The Jungle Book* a holiday box-office hit.

The success of the Disney movie did not result—fortunately, it would seem—in backing to make *King Louie the Most*. It did allow for Louis and Gia to record a Disney album, *Let's Fly with Mary Poppins*, on which the couple warbled "A Spoonful of Sugar," "Chim Chim Cher-ee," and other tunes from the Oscar-winning movie.

His popularity restored for a time with a new generation, one that was accustomed to seeing stars on television, Prima made regular appearances on shows hosted by Merv Griffin, Joey Bishop, Johnny Carson, and others. Ironically, among the biggest stars on TV was a duo who had patterned their stage act on Louis and Keely. Sonny and Cher scored pop hits with "I Got You, Babe," "The Beat Goes On," and "You Better Sit Down, Kids" and presented themselves as hip, counterculture performers. Salvatore Bono, or Sonny, eleven years older, took credit for discovering Cherilyn Sarkisian, and he wrote and arranged much of their music.

By 1969, however, after a couple of failures at the box office and a label contract ending because of dwindling record sales, Sonny and Cher had to reinvent their act and hit the nightclub circuit. That July, they had a month-long engagement at the Frontier Hotel in Las Vegas, opening for, of all people, Pat Boone, and with Sonny in a tuxedo to boot. During the gig, they found that, with Sonny playing a buffoon and Cher supplying the well-timed jibes and fine voice, the older audience embraced them.

In a *Playboy* interview, Cher recalled, "We went on the road and played nightclubs. At first, we died. Then we started getting off on the band, just getting into a little rapping, and then we noticed that people were beginning to laugh so we just started working on it. We never wrote anything down. If something worked, we'd add it, and if it didn't, we'd chuck it out."

Their act was a success on the tube too. After an appearance on *The Merv Griffin Show* in 1971, CBS created *The Sonny & Cher Comedy Hour*. It was a huge hit that ran for several years. To those watching them on television who had seen Louis and Keely a decade or more earlier, it was déjà vu all over again. Sonny and Cher also divorced, but in their case Cher went on to become a megastar.

Prima did a steady number of nightclub and theater shows, though the runs got shorter and the venues got smaller. And his energy flagged. A June 14, 1972, review in the *New York Times* of his opening at the Rainbow Grill began with a slap: "Louis Prima, lest we forget, was once a part of the jazz world." Later, the reviewer reported that after "When You're Smiling," the first number, "Mr. Prima's performance is downhill all the way. He is now a

dour, rotund man who spends most of the evening standing around while
Mr. Butera and his musicians hold the spotlight. . . . Mr. Prima's main stint is
a medley of his old recording 'hits,' an impressively forgettable list aside from
such universally performed songs as 'Just a Gigolo' and "I'm Confessin'."

While performing at the Mill Run Theatre in Chicago in the summer of
1973, the sixty-two-year-old Prima had to be helped off the stage in the middle of bellowing one of his signature songs, "When You're Smiling." Prima
was found to have suffered a mild heart attack. He began a strenuous exer-
cise program and appeared to fully recover.

Eventually, the *Jungle Book*–fueled acclaim began to ebb. He returned
to Las Vegas occasionally and even designed and constructed a golf course
there, called Fairway to the Stars, just south of the city. When he went out on
the road, he and Sam and the band found themselves in places like the Colo-
nie Coliseum Summer Theater, a small venue outside Albany, New York. In
July 1974, he told a reporter for the *Schenectady Gazette* that he never tired
of performing "as long as I can see the people."

His home base now was New Orleans, where he could always find work
and spend time with Gia and their two children. In October 1974, Mayor
Maurice "Moon" Landrieu announced a Louis Prima Week in the city. It
was a city that had changed much since he had lived there as a boy, including the razing of his home on St. Peter Street as part of the construction of a
public housing complex.

Prima began to experience headaches when he tried to sing high notes
and, before long, when he played the trumpet too. The pain increased, and
he gave up blowing the trumpet and had to keep his singing to lower ranges.
Doctors who examined him found a healthy man. But he wasn't.

"We were working at the Melody Fair in Tonawanda, New York, which
is right near Buffalo," Sam Butera recalled in a 1999 interview with the *Las
Vegas Sun*. "We were working opposite Jerry Vale. Prima was taking like
eight or nine Tylenol before each show—terrible headaches. He told me a
couple months prior, 'Sam, we're going to have to lower the keys in these
songs because I can't make those high notes anymore.' I said, 'Look, whatever you want to do, we'll do.'"

Louis began to suffer the headaches even when not performing. By the
summer of 1975 they had become intolerable, yet he continued to do shows

and record, including *Louis Prima Meets Robin Hood* for Disney and *The Wildest '75* for his Prima One label. The last song he recorded in a studio was, prophetically, "I'm Leaving You."

CAT scans were just beginning to be used, and Prima had one done of his skull. The reason for the headaches was found. "Sure enough, they saw a tumor," said Gia Prima. "It was not malignant, it was benign. But it was in the brain stem, which is the most difficult place. Every nerve in your body goes through there, so there was only one neurosurgeon who would risk it even though there would be less than 1 percent chance of survival."

In October, Prima drove to Los Angeles for an operation at Mount Sinai Hospital that would attempt to separate the tumor from the brain stem. But immediately after surgeons cut in, part of the brain hemorrhaged, and Prima went into a semicomatose state. In an especially cruel twist, he could understand and see everything around him, but he could not respond, nor could he match a thought with an action.

Four months later, Prima was flown—his fear of flying no longer mattered—to New Orleans, where he entered the Ochsner Clinic. Thus began an agonizingly slow decline to death. "He didn't ever come out of it," his sister-in-law, Madeline Prima, said about the coma in *Louis Prima: The Wildest!* "We just watched him die."

He remained in the coma, at Ochsner and then at the Touro Infirmary, for almost three years. "I went to see him once at Ochsner, and it was sad to know that he was incapacitated for so long, because in everyone's vision, Louis was indestructible, you know, and this was a monumental man," said Joe Segreto. "You just never imagined that Louis would be ill and not playing for the people."

In a 1970 interview for the New Orleans Jazz Museum, Prima was asked how he would like to be remembered. "I would like to be pictured as having a lot of fun and making people happy," he stated.

After six weeks of battling pneumonia and being given last rites, Prima died on August 24, 1978, at age sixty-seven. He was buried two days later at Greenwood Cemetery. Gia, of course, was there with her children, as was Keely with hers and first wife Louise with her daughter, Joyce. Sam Butera attended along with local musicians, some of whom dated back to the very beginning of Prima's career.

His casket was moved to a crypt in the Metairie Cemetery in 1981, on a site that, appropriately, was once a horse-racing track. On his marble tombstone is carved: WHEN THE END COMES, I KNOW, THEY'LL SAY 'JUST A GIGOLO,' AS LIFE GOES ON WITHOUT ME.

Joyce Prima lives near the site of the former Pretty Acres, the estate that her father created outside New Orleans. She had lived in New York for years and attempted a singing career of her own before returning to New Orleans for what she thought was for good. But her home and her possessions were destroyed in Hurricane Katrina in 2005, and she left the city. Pretty Acres is now the site of a Wal-Mart. Tracelene Prima returned to her native Washington State with her daughter, and Louis's second child continues to live there.

Antoinette and Luanne Prima both live in Southern California, near their mother. Toni's husband, Dennis Michaels, is an arranger and Keely's musical director. Both daughters had brushes with musical careers, which included cowriting a production in 2001 titled *The Wildest!!!: Hip, Cool and Swinging*.

Lena and Louis Prima Jr. are both singers, and they continue to perform their father's music as separate acts in nightclubs and concert halls, including Las Vegas. In interviews over the years, Lena and Louis Jr. have spoken of a happy home life. Unfortunately, both were teenagers when their father went into a coma. Their mother, Gia, no longer performs. She oversees the Louis Prima Archives, based in New Orleans, and louisprima.com. She lives in Florida. Both Gia and Keely have said repeatedly in interviews that they are writing books about their husband.

30

Life went on for Sam Butera after the Louis-Keely split. He continued with the band, which kept the name the Witnesses, and remained Louis's loyal sidekick. He did some freelancing: *Thinking Man's Sax* was one of the albums he made as a solo artist, and in 1964 he recorded *Sam Meets Sam*, a collaboration with Sammy Davis Jr., for Frank Sinatra's Reprise label. He recorded "Stargazer" with Sinatra in 1976 and that same year opened for Old Blue Eyes on a tour that included a gig at Caesar's Palace in Las Vegas. He acted in and did the music for *The Rat Race*, a Columbia feature starring two familiar Las Vegas faces, Tony Curtis and Debbie Reynolds.

Butera groused—with justification—to anyone who would listen after the David Lee Roth version of "Just a Gigolo/I Ain't Got Nobody" was released in 1985. "He copied my arrangement note for note, and I didn't get a dime for it," Sam said. He contended, however, that "there wasn't an act in Atlantic City or Las Vegas that would do that song, out of respect for me."

Alas, Butera was only a footnote in the 1996 film *Big Night*, which featured Stanley Tucci, who also cowrote the script and codirected the picture. The movie's plot is about the staff of a struggling Brooklyn restaurant that waits all night for Louis Prima to show up and eat there . . . and he doesn't. Sam's sax can be heard on the soundtrack, however.

It was only after Louis's failed operation and eventual death that Sam performed with Keely during her infrequent nightclub appearances. But they had what was described by acquaintances as a "falling-out" and ceased sharing stages.

Through the 1980s and '90s Sam continued on as a solo act. He remained popular in Las Vegas, where he and his wife, Vera, and four children had lived since 1961. According to an article titled "Lounge Wizard" in the July 13, 1997, edition of the *New York Times*, when Sam was soon to turn seventy, "Mr. Butera, who played in Mr. Prima's band and arranged many of his songs, carries on that tradition so well that he remains the highest-paid lounge performer in Las Vegas. His contract requires the kind of treatment more customary for showroom headliners: a hotel room, free meals and a provision that no other band or entertainer can perform his songs in the same building during his engagement."

But within a few years the Las Vegas lounge scene that he had helped put on the American entertainment map was fading. Sam went on the road around the country, up to forty-eight weeks a year. Then he did what some jazz artists had done much earlier in their careers—he went to Europe. There he shared stages with the likes of Van Morrison and was embraced enthusiastically by young fans who idolized his combination of swing and early rock 'n' roll. He returned to the States to play Las Vegas once more, at Sante Fe Station.

Sam's last public appearance was in 2003, when he was present to be inducted into the Italian-American Hall of Fame in New Orleans. (He had been inducted into the Las Vegas Hall of Fame four years earlier.) Then it was time to end the show for Sam: in 2004, he hung up his saxophone and declared himself retired.

Sam fell victim to Alzheimer's disease, and because of complications he was hospitalized in January 2009. He died on June 3, two months shy of his eighty-second birthday. He left behind Vera—whom he had met in high school and who was his wife for sixty-two years—his children, eight grandchildren, and one great-grandchild.

In what was both a generous homage and evidence that there was lingering animosity toward Keely, Gia said, "Louis's true ace in the hole for twenty-one years was Sam Butera. I don't care what vocalists were with Louis, his true ace in the hole was Sam Butera. Side by side, Louis and Sam kicked Las Vegas's butt for twenty-one years."

At the memorial service at St. Viator Catholic Church in Las Vegas, a longtime friend closed his eulogy by saying Butera would tell St. Peter, "I think what you should do is get rid of this guy Gabriel because I'm going to be blowing the horn from now on."

31

As of this writing, Keely Smith is still recording and performing. Hers is truly a story of survival that no one—least of all herself—could have predicted after her divorce in 1961. She may have never stopped loving Louis, but she did learn that she wasn't nothing without him.

Keely Smith didn't disappear from the entertainment scene, as that *Fabulous Las Vegas* holiday ad in 1961 implied, but it sure seemed that way. There was some solace in that she no longer had to conform to a rigorous recording and performing and traveling schedule, and she could focus on raising Toni and Luanne. As with his two previous daughters, Prima gave much more attention to his career and new family than he did to his children with Keely. She once ruefully remarked about Louis, "When he divorced the wives, he divorced the children too."

It took Keely quite a while to recover, professionally as well as emotionally, and it wasn't easy. "Louis blackballed her," contends Pete Barbutti. "He went to all the casinos and promised them that he would work for them if they didn't hire Keely. She was close to living on the street. She was going to the hotel buffets and begging."

He adds: "I believe that Shecky Greene saved her life. Shecky ran into Keely and she was in tears and looked terrible. He knew what it was like to feel very alone, and he vowed to help Keely."

"I got her back in the business," says Shecky Greene. "She wasn't getting any work, and it looked like she might not be up for it anyway, but she needed the money. The first time, I took her to open for me at a benefit for St. Joseph's Hospital in Albuquerque. Then I took her to Chicago. I said to her, 'I'll stand onstage. You don't have to get nervous. I'll even hold your hand.' And that's what I did. Keely opened her mouth, this great voice came out, and once she got going she was fine."

She made records with Dot but with mixed results and declining sales. *Swing, You Lovers, Dearly Beloved, Be My Love*, and *A Keely Christmas* were issued in 1961 and seemed to be efforts to profit from the lingering Louis and Keely popularity. Released in 1962 were *Because You're Mine*, the painfully titled *Cherokeely Swings* (with her on the cover as a squaw), *What Kind of Fool Am I?*, and *Twist with Keely Smith*, as awkward an effort as Louis's movie.

Also in '62, as Louis was hooking up with Gia, Keely made her debut as a solo performer in Las Vegas to mixed results. That same year Johnny Carson invited her to appear on *The Tonight Show,* and she sang "Little Girl Blue." Richard Rodgers saw the performance and offered her the lead in the musical *No Strings* in London, his first production since the death of his composing partner, Oscar Hammerstein II. With her children being only seven and five and the thought of living on another continent too daunting, Keely turned him down.

Europe might have been a good change of scenery, because Keely struggled with developing a career on her own. "I was scared to death at the prospect of working by myself," Keely recalled to the *New York Times* in December 1977. "In those days, I didn't express my opinion about anything. Louis told me how to look, how to dress. I never sang a song he didn't like or wear a gown he didn't like. When we broke up he told me he was going to hire another girl and call her Kelly Smith. He told me I was nothing without him. That's why I was scared. But Dinah Shore talked me into going on her television show."

Sinatra also came to the rescue. After leaving Capitol Records, Frank had established his own label, Reprise Records. He believed Keely obviously needed help to keep any kind of solo career going. He reunited her with Nelson Riddle, and together they recorded *Little Girl Blue/Little Girl New* and several songs, including "Twin Soliloquies," on a compilation album of songs from the Broadway shows *Kiss Me Kate* and *South Pacific.* Both albums were released in 1963.

Stories had circulated around Las Vegas for years about the relationship between Frank and Keely being more than friendship, even going back to 1957, when Luanne was given the middle name Francis in honor of Sinatra. As far as anyone knows, they were just stories. But Keely has acknowledged having an affair with Frank after her marriage to Louis ended.

"I almost married Frank," Keely has stated repeatedly. "He was a wonderful man, but we lived different lifestyles. Frank was on the fast lane and I was still a Virginia girl."

The arrival of the Beatles in 1964 actually boosted Keely's struggling solo career. She recorded an album, *Keely Smith Sings the John Lennon/ Paul McCartney Songbook,* that was successful in Great Britain, and a single released the following year, "You're Breaking My Heart," earned a spot in the Top 20 in England. Two more albums for Reprise followed: *The Intimate Keely Smith* and *That Old Black Magic,* in 1965 and '66.

With Sinatra out of the picture, Keely remarried in 1965 in Las Vegas. "Keely Smith, popular singer, was married today to Albert [Jimmy] Bowen, a Los Angeles recording company executive," the Associated Press reported on July 19. "About 30 persons attended the ceremony. The singer used the name Dorothy Keely Prima on the marriage license."

She essentially retired, though she termed it a hiatus, so that she could spend more time with Toni and Luanne and her new husband. But the marriage lasted less than four years. As the AP reported in May 1969, "Keely Smith, the singer, who is suing James A. Bowen, composer and conductor, for divorce, won $2,250 a month temporary support today pending trial." This came in handy, because during the last few years a struggling Louis had repeatedly fallen behind in his child support payments.

Keely married again, in 1974, to Palm Springs resident Bobby Milano, whose real name was Charles Caci. He was a supper club singer and sometime record producer who had been nicknamed the Crooning Crybaby after being convicted of complicity in jewel theft and transportation of stolen goods in 1968. He died of cancer in January 2006; the marriage had ended, but he and Keely remained friends.

In the 1970s, with her daughters on their own, Keely looked for bookings in the supper clubs of several major cities. "All of a sudden, one day, my daughters came to me and said, 'Mom, you should go back to work now,'" Keely recounted for National Public Radio in September 2007. "And I did. I finally decided one day, OK, I'll take a stab at it. They had a room at the Century Plaza hotel in Los Angeles. Joey Bishop's brother was the maitre d', and whenever an act would get sick, his brother would call and say to me, 'Keely, can you come over and fill in for us?' And I would always go do that. I thought, well, heck, this is OK, I can still do this. So I finally decided to go back to work."

She didn't have the connections in New York City as Louis did, but she was received with special warmth there when she played a three-week engagement at the Rainbow Room in 1977, her first performance in the city in fourteen years. She was well into her forties, and for one generation there was a lot of nostalgia hearing her sing "I've Got You Under My Skin" and "I Wish You Love" again, while a younger generation discovered a faded star, possibly turning her into a new one.

But Keely was not the road warrior Louis had been, and her appearances in New York, Chicago, Los Angeles, and elsewhere were too infrequent for a renewed career to gain real traction. She had reunited with Sam Butera for the Rainbow Room show, but Sam had his other projects too, and friction grew between them.

There were legal issues with Gia that must have been draining financially as well as emotionally. (Keely contended too that when she and Louis divorced, she was presented with a $130,000 bill from the IRS on revenue she never saw from her husband.) In August 1977, Keely sued a Los Angeles pawnshop. She claimed that she had sold $150,000 worth of jewelry to the shop for $24,350, but when she tried to redeem the property for over $28,000 she found that the items had been sold.

After two years of Prima being in a coma, Gia had trouble making ends meet because of the medical bills. She sought bookings in nightclubs as Gia Prima and the Witnesses, but by then, in early 1978, Keely and Sam were touring with the "real" Witnesses. Ignoring Sam's wishes, Gia argued that the name belonged to Louis's business holdings and she was the de facto head of them, so there was more legal wrangling.

Keely was still part owner of Pretty Acres, as was Gia, third wife Tracelene, Louis's brother, Leon, and his sister, Elizabeth. The property was appraised at five million dollars, and sorting out who got what took over a decade. It certainly didn't help that after his death it turned out that Louis's last will disinherited three of his six children, resulting in four of his daughters suing to have the will tossed out. There was also an argument over the disposition of the house that Louis had been building for him and Keely on the golf course in Las Vegas when they divorced. In 1995, it was purchased by Vince Neil of the rock band Mötley Crüe.

In 1985, Keely recorded an album, *I'm in Love Again*, that featured the Cole Porter title song and such other classics as "How High the Moon," "Sunday in New York," and "They Can't Take That Away from Me." But the Fantasy label release did not find an audience. David Lee Roth's version of "Just a Gigolo" put the spotlight for a time directly on Louis, and Keely remained in the shadow. The same thing happened with most of the songs that got used on movie soundtracks and advertising campaigns, such as the Gap's use of "Jump, Jive, an' Wail," because the songs were more associated with Louis than other ones he and Keely had originated or recorded in the '50s.

Keely continued to do cabaret shows here and there, in her hometown of Palm Springs (she had settled there when she married in 1974) and in Chicago, Miami, and New York. In his *Times* review of her opening night at the Rainbow and Stars in March 1991, Stephen Holden wrote, "The singer, who still wears the same Tonto haircut she had in the 1950's, balanced the playfulness with wistful renditions of several ballads that showed her voice to be in good condition. As a pop-jazz torch singer, her style has always been utterly direct and unpretentious. Performing her signature song, 'I Wish You Love,' arranged in a modified bolero style, she projected the same air of long-suffering solitude as she did three decades ago."

What began a significant change was, no surprise, because of a Palm Springs neighbor: Frank Sinatra. In 1997, Keely learned that he was seriously ill with various heart and lung ailments and was not expected to live much longer. As a gift, she wanted to make an album of her favorite Sinatra songs.

Keely had signed a contract with Concord Records, a small jazz and blues label in California, and for it she recorded an album titled *Swing, Swing, Swing*. For the Sinatra project, she went into the studio to record with the

Frankie Capp Orchestra, and among the four arrangers involved were her son-in-law, Dennis Michaels (Toni's husband), and Billy May, who had done the arrangements for her second solo album in 1958. Forty years later, they re-created the Vegas sound, and Keely's voice sounded like that of a woman much younger than sixty-nine.

After an introduction by Frank Sinatra Jr., Keely swung through eighteen of Old Blue Eyes' signature songs, including "Angel Eyes," which Frank Sr. had requested. The bulk of the recording was done on December 12, 1997, Sinatra's eighty-second birthday. Between "Angel Eyes" and "New York, New York" the musicians recorded a birthday tribute to Sinatra.

"The years passed," wrote Frank Sinatra Jr. in his liner notes. "Now, at the beginning of the twenty-first century, Keely is thinking fondly of Sinatra, her pal and soul mate, and of today's time that has left them as just two of the surviving singers of that great era. Perhaps new generations will come to know about Sinatra . . . and his faithful Indian companion, Keely, who loves and respects him as a talent, as a friend, and as an artist."

"It was truly a labor of love," said Keely about the record titled *Keely Sings Sinatra*. "Not only was Frank Sinatra a dear, dear friend, he was my love, my pal, the one I would run to when I needed a shoulder to cry on. So, some of the songs in this CD were difficult for me to sing because I knew he was sick and would not survive."

Keely sent Sinatra a copy of the CD while it was still being readied for release. He called her to say he loved it. This was their last conversation.

"I did not release this CD when it was finished because just after Frank heard it, he passed away," Keely said. "I did not want to use the publicity and jump on the bandwagon—people were coming out of the woodwork releasing Sinatra CD tributes. I was too close to Frank and loved him too much to do that."

Keely Sings Sinatra was released in 1999, and the reviews were ecstatic. For the first time since "I Wish You Love" and "That Old Black Magic," the seventy-one-year-old Keely was nominated for a Grammy Award. She did not win, but she was fully back as an artist.

Other albums followed in what became a five-record contract with the Concord label—*Keely Swings Basie Style with Strings* and *Vegas '58—Today*. The latter was recorded live at the nightclub Feinstein's at the Regency in

2004, and the *New York Observer* described it as "the most joyous show she's ever performed in New York." The show included a new version of "Oh Marie" titled "Oh Louis."

She has given a handful of interviews about her career and seems to be at peace with her years with Louis. "They were marvelous years," Keely told one writer, "filled with love, warmth, laughter, and all the nice things."

Approaching eighty, she continued to be rediscovered. It was a packed house every night for the month of April in 2007 when Keely did two shows a night at the Café Carlyle in Manhattan. On opening night Tommy Tune, Karen Akers, Phoebe Snow, and other performers were there to pay homage to a swing survivor. On another night, both Diana Krall and Bette Midler were in the audience.

Variety reported, "One only has to be on hand for 'Jump, Jive, an' Wail' to know that she has retained the ability to swing as brightly as she did with her late husband, partner and showman, Louis Prima, in their legendary lounge act a half-century ago. Smith has retained a firm, soulful voice fueled by a dusky strength. Her voice is a bold musical instrument with range and color." The nickname she had acquired during her comeback, the Queen of Swing, was more frequently invoked than ever.

According to the *New York Times*, "As the golden age of Las Vegas recedes into the gin-scented mists of Rat Pack lore, that eternal tomboy Keely Smith, now 79, is the one left standing. She is the kind of garrulous star witness dear to the hearts of showbiz historians and gossip mongers. Hers is no sob story ending in redemption. Las Vegas in '58 or thereabouts was fun, fun, fun. We should have been there."

We still are, as long as Keely keeps performing.

32

———

Over the years there have been attempts to reunite—sort of—Louis Prima and Keely Smith. The Gap came close in the mid-1990s when it sponsored commercials that featured their version of "Jump, Jive, an' Wail." Toni and Luanne gave it a shot when they collaborated with Randy Johnson and Thomas Porras on the writing of a play titled *The Wildest!!!: Hip, Cool and Swinging*. The musical had its world premiere in California on July 24, 2004, and a copy of the text is available from the publisher Samuel French Inc.

A musical titled *Louis & Keely*, created by Jake Broder and Vanessa Claire Smith, opened in June 2008 in Los Angeles to excellent reviews. It tells the story of their relationship and "The Wildest" through Louis's memory as he lies in the coma. Film director Taylor Hackford—whose work includes the Ray Charles biopic *Ray*—was involved for a time but then left the project. The production closed in November 2009, and producers made plans for a national tour. That July, a cast CD was released to strong reviews.

But the only reunion that truly mattered was a real one that happened just once, between Louis and Keely themselves. In 1971, with his career losing steam once more as *The Jungle Book* bump flattened out, Prima seized upon what he thought was a surefire cure—he and Keely would get back together. It worked once, why not try it again?

True, it had been ten years since they had last performed together, and a lot had changed in American entertainment since then, but there had to be enough people who were nostalgic for the couple—especially in Las Vegas— to make a comeback possible. The timing was perfect because a big hit on TV was *The Sonny and Cher Comedy Hour*, and it was being pointed out repeatedly that the young duo had modeled their stage dynamic on Louis and Keely.

The problem, however, was that the fast divorce in 1961 had only initiated years of fighting over money and, of course, there had been Louis's public dismissals of Keely's role in the success of "The Wildest." In a cable wired to Earl Wilson, a *New York Post* columnist, in 1962, Prima stated, "I have no desire whatsoever to have any dealings with Keely Smith under any conditions. There is nothing in the world or no one that could ever make me accept this woman in our act."

But with every passing year, Louis learned—or relearned—how important a role Keely had played with her genuine gifts. He wrote her letters, claiming that working together again would revive both their careers.

While this was probably true, Keely refused. She contended that she continued to feel hurt by his actions during their last year together, and she still had feelings of betrayal and was still smarting over Louis's arrogance toward her and lack of generosity during the last ten years. And in any case, she wanted to continue staying home with the two daughters that he had overlooked often in favor of his new family.

But Louis and Keely did indeed have one more live performance together left in them. Louis's letters became more pleasant over the next two years . . . and persuasive.

In November 1973, Prima and Sam Butera and the Witnesses were booked at Harrah's in Reno. They were performing in the lounge, with Eddy Arnold the headliner in the main room. It was opening night. Keely was in the audience. She had let Louis know that she would be at Harrah's but claimed it would be to see Arnold, not him. It seemed more likely that Keely wanted to scope out the act and see if she could fit back into it.

Still sharp-eyed with an audience, Louis spotted her during a song, and when it was over he introduced her. A spotlight sought her out, and the crowd erupted in applause. "Babe, come on up!" Louis brayed.

Nervously, yet urged on by the delighted audience, Keely went up onto the stage. The band launched into "That Old Black Magic." Keely was tentative at first, then suddenly it was as though they had just performed it the night before. Both sounded wonderful.

The crowd stood and cheered. "The Wildest" was back! It felt as if Louis and Keely had never parted. They clicked together just as though they were at the Sahara in 1958 and it was 2:00 A.M. Go on from here and it would be one of the best comeback stories in American entertainment—just think if Dean Martin and Jerry Lewis had ever reconciled. The prototype for Sonny and Cher was back in business. Just imagine how they would be greeted back on the Strip, where there was more money to be made than ever.

Louis beamed. Sam's face was split in the widest grin possible, and he prepared the band to do another number. Louis could envision that, against all odds and about to turn sixty-three, he had still one more act to go.

Keely knew she could sure use the financial benefits of a comeback too, and it was right here for the taking. But as the audience shouted for more, it all came crashing down on her. The recognition that the old black magic between them that began in a Virginia Beach dance hall twenty-five years ago was still there and might well never die was overwhelming.

She began sobbing. The audience groaned as Keely fled the stage.

She and Louis never appeared onstage together again. Their act and the love story that was a part of it became history. Over a quarter-century later, Keely regretted that her emotions had gotten the better of her. When interviewed by David Kamp for his *Vanity Fair* article, she said, "It shouldn't have ended the way it did. It didn't need to. Sometimes I wish I'd had enough sense to try to keep it up. It would have made sense."

Instead, for Louis Prima and Keely Smith, an incomparable duo who enchanted Las Vegas during its golden age, life for them was like the title of a song on their album *The Call of the Wildest*: "There'll Be No Next Time."

POSTSCRIPT

———

The 2010 New Orleans Jazz and Heritage Festival featured some of the best acts in music: B. B. King, the Allman Brothers Band, Van Morrison, Aretha Franklin, Simon and Garfunkel, Pearl Jam, a wide range of hometown talent led by the Neville Brothers and Dr. John . . . and Louis Prima and Keely Smith.

No, Louis hadn't climbed out of his crypt in the Metairie Cemetery to play pretty for the people one more time, but the more superstitious spectators in New Orleans might have thought so. On the second and last weekend of the festival, Louis Prima Jr. shook the crowd up with the same kind of infectious fun and stagecraft that had been his father's trademarks. He wore a brown pinstripe suit, a hot pink shirt, and a smile that wouldn't quit as he and his band swung through "Jump, Jive an' Wail," "Angelina," and, at the end, "When the Saints Go Marching In." His mother, Gia, had to be very proud, and a bit wistful.

The festival was dedicated to Louis Prima in honor of his centennial. He would have turned one hundred in December 2010, and the city where he was born wanted every music lover to know that Louis was one of their own, an original artist who brought more glory to New Orleans music. An admirer of his, Tony Bennett, had painted the official festival portrait of Louis, and no doubt as Bennett did so he thought of that golden age in Las Vegas when "The Wildest" made audiences shout for more.

Generously, the festival organizers extended an invitation to Keely Smith. She had just turned eighty-two, but nothing would stop her from being in New Orleans to honor Louis and to remind his fans how important she was in his life and career. Apparently, it was too much to ask that she and Louis's son perform together, so they did separate shows, with Keely performing the opening weekend. That was good news for the audience, having two acts full of that old black magic.

Keely sang that song as well as "You Go to My Head" and "Just a Gigolo" (with the crowd singing along) and other tunes that had elevated her and Louis to one of the most entertaining acts in American music. Her hair was still dark and short, and dressed in a scarlet jacket she was easy to see from a distance. The *New Orleans Times-Picayune* music critic in attendance, Doug MacCash, described Keely's voice as "smooth as a calm day on the Bayou St. John."

He added about her performance: "It was transporting. I felt like I was really in touch with the era, hearing it how it ought to be done."

When asked afterward about how she and Louis first worked together, Keely replied, "What evolved is, we fell in love. And then you can sing anything, folks."

But she proved that April afternoon that no one could sing it like Louis Prima and Keely Smith.

ACKNOWLEDGMENTS

_____

My first expression of gratitude goes to Bridget Warner LeRoy, who, as usual, knew what was good for me better than I did and introduced me to the life and music of Louis Prima and Keely Smith.

My next thanks go to Garry Boulard. He was the first writer to produce a book exclusively on Louis Prima, in 1986, titled _Just a Gigolo: The Life of Louis Prima_. He conducted interviews and did extensive research, and for those interested in knowing more about Prima's career before and after his collaboration with Smith, I highly recommend Boulard's updated edition, _Louis Prima_, published in 2002. Also very helpful to me was the 1999 documentary _Louis Prima: The Wildest!_, which can be found on DVD. It contains footage of and interviews with people no longer with us who were important in Prima's life. For the quotes from the film that I would otherwise not have been able to include in this book I am grateful to the co-owner of Historic Films, Joe Lauro, who sure knows his music. His new visit to the Chief is titled _Louis Prima: In Person_, which had its debut at the New Orleans Jazz and Heritage Festival in April 2010.

I am indebted to those who agreed to be interviewed for this book and contributed anecdotes, especially Pete Barbutti, Jack Carter, Michael Dastoli, Paul Ferrara, Shecky Greene, Lorraine Hunt-Bono, Debbie Reynolds, and Connie Stevens. Others whose recollections were useful include Tony

Bennett, Tony Curtis, Eddie Fisher, Lena Horne, Shirley MacLaine, Tony Martin, Don Rickles, and Nancy Sinatra.

Among the research sources I found most helpful were the University of Nevada at Las Vegas (thanks especially to Su Kim Chung, Kelli Luchs, and Tony Davis), Elizabeth Sherwood and Greg Lambousy at the Louisiana State Museum, Ed Berger at the Institute of Jazz Studies at Rutgers University, Bruce Raeburn at the William Ransom Hogan Jazz Archive at Tulane University, the New York Public Library, the Louis Prima Archives in New Orleans (especially Ron Cannatella and Gia Maione Prima), the Sahara Hotel Collection, the New Orleans Jazz Museum, the New Orleans Public Library, the Earl K. Long Library at the University of New Orleans, the Las Vegas City Library, the Los Angeles Public Library, the Nevada Historical Society, and the friendly staffers at the East Hampton Library, who enjoyed finding material for me almost as much as I did.

There were people who were helpful to me in various ways during the writing of this book, and I am glad to have this opportunity to thank them: Joan and Fred Baum, John and Corinne Bonfiglio, Heather Buchanan, Judge Edward Burke, Lacey Chemsak, Rosemarie Cerminaro, Stephen Dale, Bob Drury and Denise McDonald, Michael and Shelly Gambino, Joan Geroch, Michael Griffith, Nancy Hamma-Clavin, Bruce Fessier, Valerie Hanley, John Kaye, Steve Kelly, Phil Keith, Andrew Leff, David List, Chris Mitchum, Ken Moran, Kelly Olsen, Danny Peary and Suzanne Rafer, Tina Piette, Mark Rupp, Tony and Patty Sales, Megan Saboura, Lynne Scanlon, Bob Schaeffer and Fred Smith, Val and Min-Myn Schaffner, Don Sharkey, Harold Shepherd and Arlene Friedman, Ruth Simring, Nat Sobel, Mike Weatherford, and Hugh Wyatt.

Gratitude goes to Yuval Taylor, Lisa Reardon, Mary Kravenas, and others at Chicago Review Press, and the people at RLR Associates who initially believed in this project: Scott Gould, Bob Rosen, and Jennifer Unter.

My final thanks go to Nancy Bartolotta, Gertrude Clavin, and James Clavin and, as always, to my children, Brendan Clavin and Kathryn Clavin, who brought magic into my life.

SELECTED BIBLIOGRAPHY

———

BOOKS

Balboni, Alan. *Beyond the Mafia: Italian Americans and the Development of Las Vegas.* Reno: University of Nevada Press, 1996.

Basten, Fred E., and Charles Phoenix. *Fabulous Las Vegas in the 1950s: Glitz, Glamour & Games.* Santa Monica, CA: Angel City Press, 1999.

Bego, Mark. *Cher: If You Believe.* New York: Cooper Square Press, 2001.

Bennett, Tony. *The Good Life: The Autobiography of Tony Bennett.* New York: Atria Books, 1998.

Bergreen, Laurence. *Louis Armstrong.* New York: Broadway Books, 1997.

Birkbeck, Matt. *Deconstructing Sammy: Music, Money, and Madness.* New York: Amistad, 2008.

Bisso, Ray. *Jelly Roll Morton and King Oliver.* Fairfield, CA: 1st Books Library, 2001.

Boulard, Garry. *Louis Prima.* Urbana: University of Illinois Press, 2002.

Brothers, Thomas. *Louis Armstrong's New Orleans.* New York: W. W. Norton, 2006.

Calloway, Cab. *Of Minnie the Moocher and Me*. New York: Thomas Y. Crowell, 1976.

Chung, Su Kim. *Las Vegas—Then and Now*. San Diego, CA: Thunder Bay Press, 2007.

Curtis, Tony, and Peter Golenbock. *American Prince: A Memoir*. New York: Harmony Books, 2008.

Didion, Joan. *Play It As It Lays*. New York: Farrar Straus & Giroux, 1970.

Firestone, Ross. *Swing, Swing, Swing: The Life and Times of Benny Goodman*. New York: W. W. Norton, 1993.

Fisher, Eddie. *Been There, Done That: An Autobiography*. New York: St. Martin's Press, 1999.

Freedland, Michael. *Andre Previn*. London, UK: Ebury Press, 1991.

———. *Dean Martin: King of the Road*. London, UK: Robson Books Ltd., 2004.

Fischer, Steve. *When the Mob Ran Vegas: Stories of Money, Mayhem and Murder*. Omaha, NE: Berkline Press, 2005.

Gavin, James. *Stormy Weather*. New York: Atria Books, 2009.

Giddins, Gary. *Satchmo: The Genius of Louis Armstrong*. New York: Doubleday, 1988.

Hilbert, Robert. *Pee Wee Russell: The Life of a Jazzman*. New York: Oxford University Press, 1993.

Horne, Lena, and Richard Schickel. *Lena*. New York: Doubleday, 1965.

Kelley, Kitty. *His Way: The Unauthorized Biography of Frank Sinatra*. New York: Bantam Books, 1986.

Knepp, Don. *Las Vegas: The Entertainment Capital*. Menlo Park, CA: Lane Publishing Co., 1987.

Land, Barbara, and Myrick Land. *A Short History of Las Vegas*. Reno: University of Nevada Press, 1999.

Levy, Shawn. *King of Comedy: The Life and Art of Jerry Lewis*. New York: St. Martin's Press, 1997.

———. *Rat Pack Confidential*. New York: Doubleday, 1998.

Lewis, Jerry, with James Kaplan. *Dean & Me (A Love Story)*. New York: Doubleday, 2005.

Lombardo, Guy, with Jack Altshul. *Auld Acquaintance*. New York: Doubleday, 1975.

MacLaine, Shirley. *My Lucky Stars: A Hollywood Memoir*. New York: Bantam Books, 1995.

Maguire, James. *Impresario: The Life and Times of Ed Sullivan*. New York: Billboard Books, 2006.

Martin, Tony, and Cyd Charisse. *The Two of Us*. New York: Mason/Charter, 1976.

Masselli, Joseph, and Dominic Candeloro. *Italians in New Orleans*. Charleston, SC: Arcadia Publishing, 2004.

Meeker, David. *Jazz in the Movies: A Guide to Jazz Musicians 1917–1977*. New York: Da Capo Press, 1982.

Moehring, Eugene P. *Resort City in the Sun Belt*. Reno: University of Nevada Press, 2000.

Morris, Ronald. *Wait Until Dark: Jazz and the Underworld, 1880–1940*. Bowling Green, OH: Bowling Green University Popular Press, 1980.

Newton, Wayne, and Dick Maurice. *Once Before I Go*. New York: William Morrow, 1989.

Prima, Antoinette, and Luanne Prima, Randy Johnson, and Thomas Porras. *The Wildest!!!: Hip, Cool and Swinging*. New York: Samuel French Inc., 2001.

Reich, Howard, and William M. Gaines. *Jelly's Blues: The Life, Music, and Redemption of Jelly Roll Morton*. New York: Da Capo Press, 2003.

Rickles, Don, with David Ritz. *Rickles' Book: A Memoir*. New York: Simon and Schuster, 2007.

Scherman, Tony. *Backbeat*. Washington, DC: Smithsonian Press, 1999.

Shaw, Arnold. *The Street That Never Slept*. New York: Coward McCann, 1971.

Sinatra, Nancy. *Frank Sinatra: My Father.* New York: Doubleday, 1985.

Spada, James. *Peter Lawford: The Man Who Kept Secrets.* New York: Bantam Books, 1991.

Stenn, David. *Bombshell: The Life and Death of Jean Harlow.* New York: Doubleday, 1993.

Summers, Anthony, and Robbyn Swan. *Sinatra: The Life.* New York: Knopf, 2005.

Sylvester, Robert. *No Cover Charge.* New York: Dial Press, 1956.

Weatherford, Mike. *Cult Vegas.* Las Vegas, NV: Huntington Press, 2001.

NEWSPAPERS AND MAGAZINES

The archives of dozens of daily, weekly, and monthly publications were scanned for relevant information. Most useful were:

Billboard	*New Orleans Tribune*
Chicago Tribune	*Newsweek*
Downbeat	*New York Daily News*
Esquire	*New Yorker*
Fabulous Las Vegas	*New York Herald Tribune*
High Fidelity	*New York Post*
Holiday	*New York Times*
International Musician	*Oakland Tribune*
Las Vegas Review-Journal	*Offbeat*
Las Vegas Sun	*Pageant*
Life	*Philadelphia Inquirer*
Los Angeles Times	*San Francisco Examiner*
Metronome	*Time*
Miami Herald	*TV Reporter*
New Orleans Magazine	*Vanity Fair*
New Orleans Item	*Variety*
New Orleans Times-Picayune	*Washington Star*

ELECTRONIC SOURCES

Hey Boy! Hey Girl!. The Video Beat, 1995

Louisprima.com

Lvstriphistory.com

Louis Prima—The Chief, WYES-TV, New Orleans, 1983

Louis Prima: The Wildest!, Blue Sea Productions, 1999

Thunder Road, Sony Pictures Home Entertainment, 2006

Twist All Night, Keelou Corps., 1961

"You and Me": Louis Prima & Keely Smith, Cina-Music Ltd., 2000

INDEX

———